*Evergreens for Your Garden*

# Evergreens for Your Garden

by

DOUGLAS BARTRUM

JOHN GIFFORD LIMITED
125 CHARING CROSS ROAD
LONDON, W.C.2

*First published 1967*



*Printed in Great Britain*
*by Ebenezer Baylis and Son, Ltd.*
*The Trinity Press, Worcester, and London*

# Contents

# PREFACE

IN THIS little book I have attempted to describe some of the evergreen shrubs and trees which are available for growing in our gardens. Apart from hedges (of Privet, Laurel, Holly and Yew), there are comparatively few evergreen shrubs grown. And fewer trees – there are not many of these, however, to choose from (excluding the conifers); and none vies in beauty with any of the leaf-shedding, or deciduous kinds.

The shrubs are best for restricted spaces; and the smallest of the evergreen *Rhododendron* family perhaps the wisest choice for a good show. These plants, although lime-haters, can now be grown successfully in prepared beds of soil (made up of sifted peat or leaf-mould and sand), and in soils treated with lime-neutralizing agents obtainable from seedsmen and chemists. On the other hand, there are many evergreens which give a longer display of flowers and will thrive in any ordinary garden soil. And doubtless busy gardeners will consider these more suitable. For a labour-saving garden (which nowadays everybody wants), low-growing, compact shrubs, which cover the soil completely and prevent weeds from seeding and springing up, are ideal plants to grow. I have described many of the best of these in various chapters; and here and there I have quoted approximate prices of different plants, which might prove helpful to people who are planning a new garden and have only a limited sum to spend on shrubs and trees.

Most of the plants are listed in current catalogues; and many large specimens for immediate effect are obtainable – these are more expensive of course than the small pot-grown plants which are normally sent out.

All gardeners like to experiment, but they don't want to spend money on plants which may be too tender for their district, or require a special kind of soil, or some special situation. There is a large number of these amongst evergreen shrubs and trees, and in a book this size it is possible to describe only a few. They will be found under Section 2 of the last chapter; and I have chosen mostly those I know best and have seen growing in different parts of the country – several were in pots or tubs and had to be housed during bad spells of weather.

There are some remarkably fine collections of evergreens in our old country gardens. One of the most famous is at Cliveden, near Taplow, Bucks. I am greatly indebted to Mr. F. P. Copcutt for permitting me to use sprays from some of the evergreens grown there as models for the drawings in this book. Finally I wish to thank Miss Jane Timber for the illustrations she has done.

D. B.

Marlow, Bucks.

# INTRODUCTION

AN EVERGREEN retains its leaves all the year round. It is the reverse of the deciduous plant, which loses them in the autumn. Those gardeners who grow a variety of evergreens will have noticed however that some lose their leaves after a year or two. The Privet, for example, sheds them after a year; they fall in the summer as the new ones appear. There are evergreen Oaks which retain their leaves from 2 to 5 years, then shed them. And in the Pine family, the leaves (needle-like) of *Pinus aristata* and *P. balfouriana*, to mention only two, persist from 12 to 18 years. (Both species are natives of California.)

There are also semi-evergreens. These shed their leaves during exceptionally cold weather and when grown in unfavourable districts. *Buddleia globosa* (described as partially evergreen), a native of Chile and Peru, often loses all its leaves in cold northern gardens. And *B. officinalis*, from China, prospers only in warm, southern countries and is then usually evergreen.

Eventually all kinds renew their leaves, some of the oldest falling each year, while new ones are produced at the tip of each branch.

The most magnificent, the most striking of all evergreen shrubs and trees are the broad-leaved kinds that grow in the tropics, especially in the vast rain forests, where the moist, festering leaf-soil and the atmospheric conditions are ideal. Their leaves grow to an enormous size – thick, leathery leaves, very different from those of the deciduous plants that grow in our temperate zone.

The ideal place for hardy large-leaved evergreens in cultivation is a region which has an equable climate and an abundance of moisture in the soil and the atmosphere. One thinks immediately of south-west Ireland and the south-west coast of Scotland; and in gardens in these regions one comes across the finest specimens.

In the cold bleak regions of the world, and in the arctic, evergreens are chiefly conifers (cone-bearing shrubs and trees), whose leaves are often needle-like or mere scales and thus have an exceedingly small surface to expose to cold, drying winds; the plants are therefore able to survive the worst frosts, winds and snow.

None of the big-leaved evergreens such as *Rhododendron giganteum* (from the high, open forests of S.W. Yunnan) flourishes in or around the Thames Valley, since in this district there are frequent droughts in summer and long, cold, wet, frosty spells in winter and early spring; these glorious exotic plants will grow only in protected gardens in places like Cornwall and Devon. Even some of the conifers (the Christmas Tree, *Picea abies* is one) seldom thrive in many of our dry, inland gardens; they can tolerate the cold and frost; but frequent dryness at the roots causes the trees to grow weak and feeble. The finest, strongest specimens, with good thick branches, come from those regions where the rainfall is highest.

To grow evergreens successfully, especially the best of the ornamental flowering kinds, it is essential to have the right soil for them, and for the choicest a position sheltered from cold winds and frosts. One can do nothing about atmospheric conditions – one can only spray and water the large-leaved Rhododendrons and Camellias which often need it; but if one lives in a hilly, exposed district, where the soil is starved and thin, it is best not to attempt to grow the rarer kinds at all.

Gardeners who will be most successful are those who live in warm, maritime districts in the south and south-west of these islands. And fortunate indeed are those who garden in the moist, lush valleys of south-west Ireland; for there they can grow many of the large-leaved Rhododendrons and even the fragrant Mimosa – shrubs which in most parts of England are seldom seen outside the greenhouse.

But there is a vast number of hardier things which thrive in practically every garden – after all, many fine specimens of hybrid Camellias grow outside at Kew Botanical Gardens; many lovely Heathers prosper in gardens around London; and the red-flowered winter varieties, well grown and flourishing, are worth any number of rarer evergreens languishing in gardens where they obviously should never have been planted.

It is always wise before ordering any rare shrubs or trees to find out which kinds are best suited to the district where they are to be grown. Nurseries are glad to advise their customers on matters of cultivation and maintenance.

The modern garden on the whole is small and could not accommodate any of the biggest evergreens such as some of the old hardy hybrid Rhododendrons or, say, a fully-grown Silver Fir or a Blue Cedar, shrubs and trees common enough in the large pleasure-gardens of the past. But there are plenty of smaller kinds suitable for limited spaces. There are, for example, the evergreen Japanese Rhododendrons (better known as Azaleas), and many dwarf Conifers which are often grown in rock-gardens. In fact there is now an extraordinary wide variety of small compact evergreens available. New hybrid Heathers and enough of them to provide patches of brilliant colour all through the year and, moreover, Heathers which don't mind ordinary garden soils – as is well known, the vast majority in their natural habitats flourish only in peaty, lime-free ground.

Most of the low-growing compact evergreens may be described as labour-saving plants, since they grow close to the ground and thus prevent weeds seeding there and shooting up. Nothing could be more acceptable to the busy modern gardener.

What there *is* a shortage of are hardy evergreen climbers. In my opinion our native Ivy is a beautiful and very useful plant; its use in the garden is decried however by many people probably because of the plant's invasive character and its insidious habit of covering everything near it. I think it is charming on walls; incidentally it makes a fine dark background for many flowering shrubs; and the variegated and the large-leaved kinds are delightful for covering bare ground under trees. The Ivy is perhaps the only truly hardy evergreen climber we grow. I have the so-called Japanese Honeysuckle (*Lonicera japonica*) growing among shrubs in my garden, where it proves to be evergreen, and it carries its deliciously fragrant flowers over an exceptionally long period. I have had it in bloom as late as November.

But these two climbers don't appeal to everybody. After all, there are plenty of deciduous kinds which are far more beautiful.

And of all the evergreen plants we can grow in our gardens, very few approach the hybrid Rhododendrons in floral beauty and usefulness. The busy man who can spend only a short time gardening will doubtless make them his first choice.

## CHAPTER ONE

# *What the Rhododendron Family has to Offer Us*

IT IS the ambition, I think, of every garden-lover to grow some of the showy hybrid Rhododendrons. We see them perhaps in other gardens, or perhaps at one of the flower-shows – in the latter place in full bloom of course, and with perfect flowers which captivate us and make us determined to grow a specimen or two in our own gardens.

PINK PEARL, for instance, with its large rose-pink flowers carried in conical trusses, and its attractive evergreen leaves (they are very ornamental when the flowers have dropped) is one many people want. It is regarded as the most popular hybrid raised (it received an Award of Merit as long ago as 1897); there is still a great demand for it and it is among the most amenable of all the hardy hybrids.

Give it the right soil and tend it carefully during the first few years, and it will flourish luxuriantly in practically any garden. It would be a good plan to grow three together (if you have the room) to give a more striking colour effect.

To see a bed of them (a dozen or more) in full bloom in May is a spectacle which arrests one's attention and settles one's doubts about the choice of flowering shrubs for one's own garden. With a dark background, say, an evenly clipped Yew hedge (glowing rose-pink against black-green) you have a perfect picture. Or, just as enchanting: a wide grass walk flanked by single rows of the shrubs, with Yew hedges at the back.

For most of the year there will be just the foliage: the charming light green of the Rhododendrons, so dense that no ground can be seen (and no weeds can root); and behind, the close compact contrasting green of the Yew.

'All right for the large, old-fashioned garden,' you might say; 'but what about the small modern garden?'

In the smallest plots it is possible to find room for one plant. PINK PEARL grows slowly (though strongly) and quite small specimens can be bought. (Cost in 1966 was about 28*s*. for the smallest plant.) It could occupy a bed (circular shaped preferably) on its own, either in the middle of a small lawn, or perhaps in a place in a border along with other shrubs. It would probably do better in the border, since it would get a little more shade there than in the middle of a lawn. Full shade is not necessary for many of the old hardy Rhododendrons (familiarly known as the 'Iron-clads'); but the colours are inclined to bleach when exposed to sun all day long – this is especially true of the mid-summer blooming varieties: those that are at their best at the end of June, say.

PINK PEARL is one of the hardy hybrids I recommend for the average garden in this country.

Before considering any other varieties, let us look at the problems of planting and cultivation in general. (There's nothing exceptionally difficult to tackle.)

Rhododendrons and Azaleas need a lime-free soil. If you garden on chalk, that is, if you find chalk boulders in your soil – even if they're a good distance down – , it isn't worth trying to grow these shrubs at all. A moist lime-free soil is of paramount importance in their cultivation.

It is seldom possible, however, by just digging to ascertain whether your soil contains lime or not (the presence of chalk boulders is an extreme case). But it is possible to have the soil tested by sending a specimen to a nursery which undertakes the work, or to one of the agricultural research stations. They will advise you. Or you can do the job yourself with a Lime-testing set which can be bought at any good horticultural stores.

It will be difficult, I think, to find the ideal soil in the vast majority of our gardens; but soils can be treated and improved. The natural way is to incorporate plenty of coarse sand and peat or leaf-mould with heavy clay; and plenty of peat with light soils. (I use three parts of sifted leaf-mould to one part of my lightish sandy soil, which is slightly limy, and put a 6-inch layer of leaf-mould (or decayed leaves, when I can get them) and some sand round the shrubs regularly every April.) This top layer or mulch is thus continually renewed, the old rotting layers feeding the roots which of Rhododendrons and Azaleas lie near the surface of the ground.

The artificial way is to feed the soil with the chemical preparation known as Murphy Sequestrene, which is obtainable at any chemist's. It is a chelating agent, *chelation* being the chemical inactivation of the calcium or lime in the soil. Thus it is possible to grow calcifuge (lime-shy) plants in chalky soils. The treatment should be repeated yearly.

What is the best time for planting hybrid Rhododendrons? April, most professional gardeners say. It is wise to order them some months ahead so that you get them in time. I've always planted mine in mid-April (a month when the sap is active); and I've got the nurserymen to spray the plants with the new plastic spray which retards the loss of moisture during the 'shock' period of transplanting and re-establishment. The evergreen leaves do not wilt so readily when they have been thus treated. Furthermore it is very necessary to keep the plants well watered during dry spells; and they should also be sprayed overhead as frequently as possible during the hot summer.

The actual planting is a straightforward job: dig a hole big enough to take the roots comfortably when they are spread out. With Rhododendrons however the ball of roots is intact and well covered with good leafy soil as a rule.

Firm the bottom of the hole, put the plant in, taking great care that the base of the stem or trunk is not below the surface of the ground. Fill up with a mixture of three parts of sifted leaf-mould or peat and one part of coarse sand. Press the soil well down round the roots – or even tread on it to make it firm: you cannot plant Rhododendrons too firmly. And if the weather is dry, keep the soil moist by watering regularly till the rains come. Rain water or soft water is best for these plants.

As regards the site: a partially shady one is best for all types of Rhododendrons. The owner of a small garden hasn't much choice perhaps, and if his garden is in an exposed position, he would be wise to plant one or two standard trees to provide some shade during the sunniest part of the day. The small-leaved varieties (belonging to the *Lapponicum* Series, or Group) are better for a sunny position than the large-leaved kinds. Small plants such as the hybrids BLUE BIRD, BLUE TIT, and the semi-evergreen PRAECOX are often planted against boulders in the rockery, where they get a certain amount of shade.

PRAECOX eventually makes a moderate-sized spreading shrub, but may be pruned back to keep it fairly small. The so-called

Japanese Azaleas (evergreen) will certainly benefit from the shade and protection afforded by the rocks.

Most nurseries have good stocks of Rhododendrons. Hillier; Slocock; Reuthe; Waterer of Bagshot; are some of the best known specialists and list hundreds of different varieties in their catalogues. The newest varieties seem less hardy than the very old ones and in some districts may need protection during bad winters.

The old 'Iron-clads' are obtainable from the nurseries I've mentioned above and will no doubt appeal to people whose gardens are in high, exposed places. A word of warning, however: many grow to an enormous size and are therefore quite unsuitable for small gardens.

A number of them may be seen at Kew Botanic Gardens and in some of the pleasure gardens of the great houses, which are often open to the public. LADY DE ROTHSCHILD, with white flowers flushed with carmine, is a gigantic shrub at Kew; it towers above one and leaves one feeling a little uncertain about the suitability of the other old hybrids. There are plenty of moderate-sized ones among them, however, and they're all hardy enough for the average garden in this country.

I give a list here of all kinds – old and new – , though not just a catalogue-list, which makes tedious reading.

A famous raiser of hybrid Rhododendrons when once asked to name what he considered to be the finest hardy kinds for the garden, gave the following:

BLUE PETER
BRITANNIA
CORONA
EARL OF ATHLONE
FASTUOSUM FLORE PLENO
LADY CLEMENTINE MITFORD
LETTY EDWARDS
MOUNT EVEREST
SOUVENIR DE ANTHONY WATERER
SOUVENIR OF W. C. SLOCOCK
UNIQUE

He didn't include PINK PEARL or OLD PORT, two special favourites of mine; but no doubt the ones mentioned were those he grew and had got to love. Several make medium-sized shrubs – room could be found for three probably in the smallest garden.

The eleven are included in and described with my selection.

ALBUM ELEGANS. This is a very old hybrid which was raised by Waterer's of Bagshot, and seems to be a little difficult to get

1. Hybrid Rhododendrons massed prevent weeds springing up.

2. Pink Pearl—the best known of all the evergreen hybrid Rhododendrons.

3. *Berberis Darwinii*—a hardy evergreen shrub with striking orange-coloured flowers.

4. *Cistus x Purpureus*—An easy evergreen to grow in a warm district.

nowadays – you might have to go to Waterer's for it. The name is odd, since the flowers are not white (ALBUM means white), but an exquisite pale mauve which fades to white. It is tough and completely hardy, tall-growing, and has been used very effectively as a screen and as a hedge, and also as a background to smaller Rhododendrons. It blooms in late May around London – earlier in the south.

AUGFAST. A smallish shrub not more than 4 feet tall as a rule and therefore suitable for limited spaces. It doesn't like full sun, however, and should be given the front position in a partially-shady border. Set three together, if you can: two in front, 4 feet apart, and one behind; you will get a lovely splash of dark lavender-blue, in May. The name AUGFAST is derived from the names of the species which produced the shrub, viz. *R. fastigiatum* and *R. augustinii*; the latter, by the way, has the bluest flowers of all the Rhododendron species. An excellent shrub to plant with AUGFAST is the evergreen *Mahonia aquifolium*. (See page 31.) Plant several: some behind as a background, and one or two on each side of the Rhododendron.

ASCOT BRILLIANT is another of the old hardies, with brilliant red flowers, which come early. Unless your garden is well protected (has a wall round it, for instance), you will need some overhead shelter to mitigate the force of north winds and give some protection from late spring frosts. But fortunately the flowers often escape. If you want to see a really fine specimen in bloom, go to Kew in April.

BARON DE BRUIN. This is an old hardy variety which blooms late. Its dark red flowers are seldom damaged by frost and the shrub itself doesn't seem to suffer when battered about by cold winds.

BLUE BIRD. (A.M. in 1943.) It is a lovely blue *augustinii* hybrid. The flowers are of an exquisite violet-blue shade, with a deeper blotch. They open in April and suffer little harm in a reasonably sheltered rock-garden. The plant looks best though, massed along the front row of a border.

BLUE PETER is considered one of the finest of the hybrids and is of medium height. Good for a small garden. The flowers are perhaps the bluest of all we can find in the hybrids. It is a mid-season bloomer. In 1933 it received an A.M. and in 1958 a First Class Certificate. Raised by Waterer's.

BLUE TIT. Another 'blue' hybrid and very suitable for small

gardens or for the rockery. It seldom reaches more than 3 feet in height, and makes a compact shrub, lovely in late April, with its smallish lavender-blue flowers springing from the tips of the branches.

BRITANNIA received a F.C.C. in 1937. It is a special favourite with Rhododendron-lovers and has beautiful crimson-scarlet, gloxiana-shaped flowers in early June. They bleach, however, if exposed to full sun.

BRIC-A-BRAC is a pure white Rhododendron, which in time makes a neat little bush about 2 feet high. The flowers open early and measure 2 inches across. It deserves a sheltered spot and we usually find it in the rock-garden. White Rhododendrons are rather rare and probably less popular than the coloured varieties.

BUTTERFLY is one of the yellow-flowered hybrids – a beautiful shrub. The colour is an exquisite lemon-yellow and each flower is blotched with deep chocolate. The flowers come freely in early May and need some shade. Very lovely massed with bluebells for a landscape effect. But you need a big garden or a woodland for it.

CHRISTMAS CHEER. A curious name for a plant which blooms in March. But perhaps not too inappropriate when March snows cover the ground. The colour is blush-pink; the flowers force well in a greenhouse but lose some of their lustre grown under glass. This hybrid makes a useful compact shrub for a small garden. In the London district it will need some overhead shelter.

CARMEN is derived from the slow-growing, prostrate species *R. repens*, whose natural habitat is the cold mountainous parts of China. A mere shrublet and therefore best in the rockery. April blooming. The flowers are of a waxy texture and crimson and bell-shaped.

CORONA. A May bloomer and does well in a tub, where I have often seen it growing and flowering profusely. There is nothing unusual about that, though; for many hybrids do well in tubs. A fine shrub for a town garden. (It prospers in London). The flowers are coral-pink. A cold, rather exposed site is good for it and seems to toughen it; in the warm south it often grows lush. Raised by Waterer's. An old favourite.

COUNTESS OF DERBY. Another old favourite and often seen massed in large gardens. A tallish shrub and very hardy. It is a cross between PINK PEARL and the rosy-crimson CYNTHIA, and is sometimes described as an 'improved PINK PEARL.'

EARL OF ATHLONE is a Dutch hybrid with rich blood-red flowers which are at their best in May. It was considered a rather tender shrub at first, but in the hands of the nurserymen it has become hardier through the course of years, the strongest-grafted plants being selected for stock and increase. It received an F.C.C. in 1938. I've seen it in full bloom with dark red tulips massed in front of it.

ELIZABETH. This is another *repens* hybrid. A low, spreading shrub with blood-red, trumpet-shaped flowers, which come in clusters. It prefers a partially shady spot and is an excellent shrub for a narrow border.

ELIZABETH HOBBIE carries large scarlet flowers in April. It is completely hardy but does best in a fairly shady position.

FAGGETER'S FAVOURITE is a hybrid of *R. fortunei*, which species is a native of Eastern China. The colour is curious: a blend of pink, cream and lavender. The flower-buds are scarlet and begin to open in May. This hybrid has attractive green foliage; it is a charming shrub for a border.

FASTUOSUM FLORE PLENO. A very old hybrid which is still obtainable, however, and is prized by most collectors. The flowers, mauve, are semi-double and are rosette-shaped. They open at the end of May.

GOLDSWORTH YELLOW has been called the best yellow hybrid Rhododendron in cultivation. If you see it in bud, the colour is apricot; but in full bloom, the flowers are an enchanting shade of primrose-yellow, the petals spotted with green and bronze.

IMPEANUM. This hybrid was raised at Kew Botanic Gardens. It is a perfect, low-spreading shrub for the rock-garden; its cobalt-blue flowers looking particularly attractive against the grey rocks. It usually blooms in late April.

LADY CLEMENTINE MITFORD. An old hardy hybrid raised by Anthony Waterer. It's at its best in early June and is medium-sized and has large trusses of flowers, their colour being a blend of pink and yellow – described by nurserymen as 'peach'.

LETTY EDWARDS was awarded an F.C.C. in 1948 and derives its yellow colour from the parent *R. campylocarpum*. Often the flowers are marked with crimson in the throat. This hybrid makes a medium-sized shrub and blooming in April really needs some overhead shelter.

LODERI. Acclaimed by all Rhododendron enthusiasts as the finest hybrid in the world! Unfortunately I can't grow it successfully in my garden in South Buckinghamshire. It needs a warmer part of England. Regarded as the King of hybrid Rhododendrons and is a truly magnificent plant. The shrub is large, the flowers are enormous, scented and measure 5 inches across individually. There are many forms of the variety; LODERI PINK CORAL, LODERI SIR EDMUND (flowers opening blush-white) are two I've seen in several gardens in Sussex (near the coast), in which county the hybrid was raised.

MARS. A tough old hardy hybrid: even so, it does better in partial shade. The colour of the flowers (June blooming) are described as pure red; there is however a touch of bronze in the colour. The plant received a F.C.C. in 1935.

MOTHER OF PEARL. This hybrid is a sport from PINK PEARL which it resembles in form and foliage. The colour is a lovely blush-pink; and it turns a pearly-white as the flowers age. They open in May.

MOUNT EVEREST. A white, delicately-scented variety of moderate size. It blooms in early May and is best in partial shade. The colour is not pure, however: there is a touch of red about the flowers.

MRS. FURNIVAL has pink flowers with a brownish blotch and a yellow eye. As the colour soon begins to fade in full sun, partial shade is necessary. As regards providing this: the spreading branches of large trees in the vicinity will usually give sufficient shade; and often a wall or a fence will.

MUM is one of the late bloomers and has white flowers with a yellow eye. It is a fine, very hardy shrub with attractive foliage and of compact habit.

MYRTIFOLIUM. One of its parents is the Alpine Rose. (*R. hirsutum*), a native of the European Alps. The hybrid is a hardy, compact little shrub with rose-pink flowers in June. A good choice for a small garden.

NOBLEANUM. If you lived in Cornwall or in the Channel Islands, you would probably have this Rhododendron in bloom at Christmas. It is among the earliest. But in the Home Counties the flowers seldom begin to open before February. But it's good and heartening to see them then, for one knows that spring is on the way. The flowers vary from pink to crimson; and NOBLEANUM ALBUM is white. They are slow-growing shrubs but eventually reach a height of about 15 feet.

OLD PORT is a special favourite of mine and I like to see it massed in a large bed on its own – in fact its curious colour (reddish-purple) clashes with most other colours. Some gardeners dislike it. For a real riot of colour, plant the brilliant orange Welsh Poppy (*Meconopsis cambrica*) near it.

OSTFRIESLAND. A hybrid from Germany: a dwarf with crimson flowers in April; a charming shrub for edging a border in partial shade.

PENJERRICK is like LODERI, suitable only for sheltered places and is almost as fine a shrub as that noble plant. 'For sheer magnificence,' says a grower, 'PENJERRICK has few rivals among flowering shrubs.' There are pink, cream and white forms of it, and they make tall shrubs which need a great deal of room.

PINK PEARL. The most popular and probably the most successful of all the many hundreds of hybrids raised. It is recommended by all nurseries and possibly seen in more gardens in this country than any other Rhododendron – hybrid or species. It is very hardy. The flowers are a deep shade of pink in the bud; slightly paler when fully open – and paler still if they are exposed to full sun. Gorgeous when massed in partial shade against a dark green background.

PRAECOX. The name means *early*. And it is one of the earliest hybrids to flower. In my garden, 30 miles west of London, I have it in full bloom during February, if the winter is mild. But more often than not it is April before the buds begin to show deep rose-pink. The leaves are small and often turn yellow and fall in cold weather – or some of them do: the plant is never leafless in this district. For a free flowering, ornamental hedge it is superb. When in full bloom, no foliage can be seen. A hedge smothered with rose-coloured blossoms. The finest in these islands is the hedge 50 yards long at Edinburgh Botanical Gardens.

PURPLE SPLENDOUR is one of the old very hardy 'Iron-clads'. The flowers are dark purple and have a black central eye or spot. It flourishes practically anywhere and blooms in early summer. Regarded as the finest purple hybrid ever raised; and one of Waterer's.

RACIL. It makes a pleasing-looking shrub about 5 feet high, which has very charming pinkish-white flowers – a deeper shade in the bud. Excellent for a small garden.

SAPPHIRE. A hybrid between BLUE TIT and *R. impeditum.* This plant resembles the latter shrub. It is of open habit, has pretty pale lavender flowers in April; and it needs some overhead shelter.

SOUVENIR DE ANTHONY WATERER. The plant is named after the eminent hybridist. It is a tall, upright shrub with deep pink flowers (with a yellow blotch) carried in big trusses. A favourite with most collectors, as is

SOUVENIR OF W. C. SLOCOCK. A primrose yellow flowered hybrid which derives its colour from the parent *R. campylocarpum.*

TESSA is a hybrid between PRAECOX and *R. moupinense.* It is sometimes described in catalogues as 'A small bush about 3 feet.' But a mature specimen is usually taller than that. It is an open bush with small purplish-pink flowers which come in February. There are several good specimens at the Savill Gardens near Windsor. The shrub needs overhead shelter.

UNIQUE. Another *R. campylocarpum* hybrid with pale ochre flowers slightly touched with peach; they open in April. It forms a tight, compact bush and is a good choice for smallish gardens.

VANESSA was raised by Lord Aberconway. It is a *griersonianum* hybrid, the first in fact that was exhibited; and it received a F.C.C. in 1929. It was acclaimed then by collectors as the loveliest of all the pinks (there are others as good now) and it blooms in May. Shelter helps to preserve the exquisite colour of the flowers and of course protect them from late spring frosts.

These are but a few of the many hundreds of hybrids obtainable. It is not an easy matter to make a choice for one's garden; and if it has to be just one or two shrubs, then the task is much more difficult. I always advise gardeners to visit the nursery where they intend buying their shrubs and see them first in full bloom. Or visit one of the Rhododendron shows.

On the whole the hybrids are hardier, tougher plants for the garden than the species, which, however, always catch my eye before the more showy hybrids. There are plenty of Rhododendron species perfectly hardy and amenable to cultivation in most of our gardens (they all have character – there is a certain natural ruggedness about them); they are all evergreen, the exceptions being most of the so-called Azaleas.

A few species were grown in some of our gardens during the

17th and 18th centuries; and from these few, the first hybrids were raised. These earliest species came from Europe – *R. ponticum*; *R. luteum* (or *Azalea pontica*) and the Alpine Roses – ; and some from North America. But the most striking, the most beautiful came to us from Asia, particularly from the mountainous regions of India and China.

I give a descriptive list of about a dozen. It is actually a Species Poll, the plants having been chosen by some of the leading specialists in the country. They are the best hardy kinds for the average garden in these islands – though one or two would be a bit of a risk, I think, in districts as far north as London.

2

*R. augustinii* (named for the botanist Augustine Henry, who discovered it in Hupeh, Southern China, at an altitude of 9000 feet). It is the bluest of all the species. You should ask for the truest blue forms when buying it: there are inferior, dull blues and nondescript shades. Unfortunately the superior ones are on the tender side and need some shelter in cold districts. This species flowers in May and usually escapes the worst frosts. It is scarcely suitable for small gardens, since it ultimately reaches a height of 10 feet; and to get a really striking effect of glowing blue, you should plant a group of the shrubs.

See them at Kew in May. They are quite startlingly beautiful. The branches are packed with 2-inch blue flowers, almost hiding the leaves. (The smallest plants cost about 30s. each.)

*R. barbatum* (the specific epithet means *barbed* or *bristly*, referring to the stems and the leaves). Although this is included as a suitable species, it certainly isn't any good in gardens in the Home Counties. Personally, I've never seen it prospering outside Devon and Cornwall and gardens on the western seaboard. It has been chosen simply for its magnificent colour. There is no red like it. It glows and astonishes you when you first see it. The dull green foliage is an excellent foil. Another point intending growers must consider: it makes a tall shrub or tree up to 15 feet in height and is not suitable for a small garden – even in the warm south. I would give anything to be able to grow it; but it does not succeed in Buckinghamshire.

*R. campylocarpum* (with bent fruits or seed-pods). Like

*R. barbatum*, this species is found growing at an altitude of 12,000 feet in the Himalaya, the ideal place for Rhododendrons, for it is well above the damp, frost and fog level, and so cold that the flower-buds remain dormant till the spring arrives. The flowers in the best forms of this species are of a clear canary yellow; they are bell-shaped, about 2½ inches across, come in clusters, and are slightly fragrant; the leaves are smallish (2 to 4 inches long) and a pleasing green colour. It is a slow-growing shrub, neat and bushy, reaching a height of from 4 to 8 feet. In exceptionally wet regions it grows lush and appears then not to flower very freely; it does best in the drier parts of this country. Many gardeners advocate disbudding the plant every second year to prevent it from exhausting itself by over-flowering. It blooms in May and I've often seen it associated with bluebells. A charming colour association: yellow above pale blue.

*R. cinnibarum* (cinnibar-red: referring to the flowers). The flowers, funnel-shaped, are a striking bright cinnibar red as a rule, and come in clusters of about 5, above the oval evergreen leaves. They bloom in early summer. The colour varies considerably, however; the yellow-orange shades are not so attractive, I think, as the red. This species reaches a height of from 6 to 10 feet and makes a thin, open shrub. Weeds soon spring up round it (it is not one of the compact weed-smothering evergreens). It should be underplanted with dwarf Heathers or with a low evergreen shrub such as the Holly-leaf *Mahonia* (*Mahonia aquifolium*). (See page 31.)

*R. discolor* (different colours). Some fine specimens may be seen at Kew. They were about 8 feet tall when I saw them a few years ago and full of flowers – in mid-July. This species is one of the last to bloom and is therefore a useful shrub to have. Unfortunately it is too big for small gardens, reaching sometimes a height of 15 feet in the south; farther north it is smaller. The flowers, funnel-shaped, large and scented, are pink or white, marked with yellow-green at the base. The shrub prefers a shady spot.

*R. fortunei* (named in honour of Robert Fortune, the famous collector, who worked in China during the 19th century). A tall evergreen, 10 to 12 feet high, though seldom that height in this country. The large flowers, blush-pink, are delightfully fragrant and open in May. The largest leaves are about 8 inches long and pale green. It is a completely hardy shrub and seems to revel in an open position in the garden. The *fortunei* race of hybrids are noted for their delicate colouring and their delicious scent.

*R. griersonianum* (named for C. Grierson, a friend of George Forest's; they collected together in China). Like the gorgeous *R. barbatum*, this species is suitable only for the warmest gardens in these islands. It is included in the list because of its glorious red colour. It is a glowing geranium red – described by some gardeners as 'a red-hot red'.

*R. hippophaeoides* (resembling sea-buckthorn). A smallish species, 4 to 5 feet high, and one of the easiest to grow. The flowers are very variable in colour; the most attractive is the blue or lavender-blue – there are deep purplish-blue, bluey-rose, and pink forms. The leaves are small (the species belongs to the Lapponicum Series); they are of a greyish tint and pleasing to see all through the year. The plant blooms in March and April and is completely hardy: certainly one for those on the look out for an easy species. It may be raised from seed and also from cuttings, these rooting very readily. The plant was discovered by Kingdon Ward in Yunnan, China, in 1913. In the wild it grows in exposed and often boggy places.

*R. kingianum* (named for Sir George King who died in 1909; he was director of the Botanic Gardens, Calcutta). Botanists regard the plant as a geographical form of *R. arboreum*. But its foliage is different, the leaves being much broader and more rounded. The flowers are a magnificent shade of deep scarlet and come in compact trusses; they open towards the end of June and can always be relied upon to give a good display.

*R. russatum* (reddened; the epithet probably refers to the reddish flower-stems). A small-leaved species and quite a dwarf – seldom more than 3 feet high, under cultivation. The flowers are a vivid purple, small and come in clusters of from 5 to 10. They bloom in April and are very striking when seen in a mass as, for example, when the shrub is used for edging a border.

*R. sutchuense* (from Szechwan, China). It was found in Western Hupeh, China, by the famous collector Wilson in 1901 and first flowered in Britain in 1910. The deep rose-pink kind (Var. GERALDII) is the most beautiful; the magenta shades of other kinds are far less pleasing – magenta in flowers isn't a favourite colour. The plant makes a rather big shrub in time (10 feet or more high) and is very fine in leaf; the leaves measure from 6 to 10 inches in length. As it blooms in March, it needs a sheltered spot.

*R. thomsonii* (named for Thomas Thomson, Superintendent of the Calcutta Botanic Gardens from 1854 to 1861). This species recommended by the specialists needs a warm, sheltered garden in the London district or the flowers will suffer (unless the weather in March, when it blooms, is exceptionally mild). Often with these precocious shrubs, the flowers open undamaged and are beautiful for a short time, then overnight are completely destroyed by a frost. Cornwall is the best place for it – or some district with a similar climate. The blood-red colour is the species' great attraction; and the leaves, sea-green, show off the flowers effectively. These are bell-shaped, measuring 2 inches across and come in loose clusters. *R. thomsonii* eventually makes a big shrub up to about 14 feet tall. It is suitable only for the largest gardens.

These are but a few of the species obtainable; most Rhododendron specialists give over a hundred in their catalogues (Hillier lists about 150); all desirable plants, all evergreen. *R. sinogrande*, with leaves 2½ feet long and 1 foot wide, is included and designated as tender and one needing shelter and a warm district.

Others (*R. radicans* and *R. repens*, for example), are prostrate creeping species only a few inches high and obviously best (and probably safest) in the rockery, among the stones.

*R. ponticum* is the mauve species we see naturalized in some of our woodlands, particularly in Surrey and Hampshire. It is not a native plant (no Rhododendron is), but is has established itself very well in many parts of the country. It is used as a game covert in woodlands and also for hedges and screens and is a favourite shrub with many gardeners. This species was introduced into Britain about the middle of the 18th century. From this and others, such as *R. maximum* (called the Great Laurel) from North America, the earliest hybrids were produced.

The scarlet *R. arboreum* is a glorious evergreen species, but tree-like and decidedly on the tender side. Around London it is best grown in a cool greenhouse. (At Kew a grand specimen is housed in the Temperate House and blooms there in February.)

There are dozens of other species. See them in bloom first, and also, before you make your choice, get as much information as you can about the plants, about their likes and their dislikes.

The owner of a small modern garden will naturally be compelled to choose the smallest kinds. Those described in the following Section are on the whole less intractable than the small wild alpine species, which, like all the wild Rhododendrons need growing conditions similar to those they get in their natural habitats – often the high mountainous regions of Europe and Asia, where there is an abundance of moisture in the soil (from melting snows) and the atmosphere; and cooling mists in the hot summer keep the foliage wet and moist.

'Remove all seed-pods or dead flower-heads,' is the advice given by growers and specialists. This is done to prevent the plants exhausting themselves through seed production. It doesn't take long to pinch them off one or two plants. In a large garden, where hundreds are growing, the job is often neglected. In the wild it is never done – the seeds drop naturally or birds devour them.

## 3

The small compact evergreen Rhododendrons (or Japanese Azaleas, as they are popularly called) give a wonderful show of blossom in May. Like some of the miniature alpine Rhododendrons, they flower so profusely that the foliage is completely hidden. In their early days, and for a year or two, they are rather tender and need a little protection and nursing during severe winter weather.

As regards soil, they like lime-free, peaty soils as do all the genus; yet it musn't be too rich for these Azaleas (use two parts of coarse sand, one part peat, and one part loam); too rich a medium causes the plants to make a lot of sappy growths, which are very susceptible to frost damage. Any deficiency in nutriment in the soil is easily supplied by yearly mulching with well rotted leaves in April.

The plants like partial shade – or most of them do – and in a small garden the best place for them is probably in a border near the house: shade and protection are supplied permanently by the walls. In exceptionally bad weather (frost and snow for days on end) the plants are effectually sheltered by cloches, or bell-glasses; they should be removed occasionally (when the sun shines) to provide ventilation. Severe and prolonged frost causes bark-splitting, which is often fatal.

The best-loved kinds are the *Kurumes*, which originated in Japan, and were derived from different Azaleas found growing on Mount Kirishima on the island of Kiushiu. Principally in the town of Kurume on the island, Japanese hybridists had worked for years on the plants, producing many beautiful garden forms, which are known to us as the *Kurume Evergreen Azaleas*, many of which were introduced by Wilson, the collector, into American and European gardens after the First World War. Close on a hundred are listed in specialists' catalogues today. As with the hybrid Rhododendrons, choice of varieties is a difficult task: one seems as beautiful as another. Many, like some Polyanthuses, have hose-in-hose flowers, that is, one flower within another.

ADDY WERY has deep red flowers and beautiful dark glossy green foliage, the leaves, as in all Azaleas, resembling those of the Box (*Buxus sempervirens*), but colouring in the autumn. The plant needs some shade or its flowers will bleach. It received an A.M. in 1950.

AYA-KAMMURI. This is one of Wilson's first introductions, grown in the Arnold Arboretum, Boston, Mass., before it came to Britain. A lovely small shrub, with rose (sometimes salmon-red) flowers touched with white.

AZUMA-KAGAMI. Deep pink flowers, hose-in-hose. The plant doesn't seem to mind full exposure (after a few years of hardening-off), provided the soil is kept moist.

CHRISTMAS CHEER. (The Japanese name is IMA-SHOJO, which is mostly used nowadays). The English name seems quite inappropriate, since the plant blooms in late April, and the flowers are a warm, bright red, hose-in-hose formed. One of the early introductions.

DAPHNE is a charming white variety (hose-in-hose). It ought to be planted in shade, not that the flowers need it more than the others, but white in a subdued light (or in shadow) is always more beautiful; in full sun it stares and can be quite hard to the eyes.

HINODEGIRI is said to be an exceptionally hardy variety. It is certainly one of the most popular. It has bright crimson flowers which are at their best in early May. This shrub was one of those (50 altogether) that Wilson saw in Japan in 1914. He chose these from the hundreds of varieties which the Japanese had raised from indigenous plants.

HINOMAYO. Among the loveliest for colour: an exquisite glowing shell pink, the flowers completely hiding the foliage. The first of the *Kurumes* that I ever saw in this part of the country. It grew in a shady dell at 'Greengates' which belonged then to Lord Hambledon. The estate is near Henley-on-Thames. Some specimens have been known to grow up to a height of 5 feet or more. The plant received an A.M. in 1921 and a F.C.C. in 1945.

HOO (a delightful name). In some catalogues the plant appears under APPLE BLOSSOM. Another of Wilson's 50. A dainty little evergreen: white flowers tinged with pink. It blooms at the end of April; it is regarded by most growers as on the tender side.

IRO-HAYAMA or DAINTY, described as *Number* 8 of Wilson's 50. It was awarded an A.M. in 1952. The colour is a rose-lavender with a whitish centre and a pale brownish eye. It has proved to be quite hardy in most gardens.

KIREN (DAYBREAK). One of the hardier varieties, of low compact growth, with rose-pink, hose-in-hose flowers. It is listed as *Number* 22 of Wilson's early collection.

SHIN-SEIKAI is very hardy and has creamy-white flowers in May (hose-in-hose).

All these shrubs ultimately make neat compact bushes from 2 to 3 feet high – HINOMAYO, as I've already mentioned, grows taller.

The wild species from which the *Kurumes* were derived were *R. obtusum*, *R. kinsuanum*, and *R. kaempferi* (formerly called Azaleas). The last-named species was crossed with a plant named *Azalea malvatica*, a shrub imported to Holland from Japan and used by hybridists there to produce some very beautiful evergreen forms. These are described now as *Malvatica X Kaempferi* hybrids, and very suitable for small gardens. I single out the following as the most beautiful. They flourish in many gardens in the London district.

ALICE. This hybrid has striking salmon-red flowers, which last longer in partial shade. It blooms in May.

BETTY. Another beauty. It blooms in May and has rich orange-pink flowers. A.M. in 1940.

EVA has rose-violet flowers; they are unusually large and come in clusters.

JEANETTE. Deep pink flowers in May.

JOHN CAIRNS is reputed to be the hardiest of these *malvatica* hybrids; it received an A.M. in 1940. It ultimately makes a tallish shrub and has brick-red flowers in May.

Another group of hardy evergreen Azaleas is the *Vuykiana* Group, so named after the Dutch Firm, *Vuyk Van Nes*, which first produced them.

Two of the best known (and they are the loveliest, I think) are a pure white and a deep red:

PALESTRINA. It is one of the hardiest of all the evergreen garden Azaleas, and with its ice-cold white flowers, truly one of the most beautiful of all small garden shrubs. The plant is best massed on its own against a dark green background. It blooms in May.

QUEEN WILHELMINA has deep vermilion-red flowers and does best in partial shade. The plant usually appears in catalogues under its German name, viz. KÖNIGEN WILHELMINA.

There are many other kinds of evergreen Azaleas; but none is any more beautiful than those I've described above. (The plants, by the way, cost about 15*s*. each).

The varieties of *R. indicum* do not seem to be as hardy as those with *kaempferi* blood in them. And the *R. simsii* hybrids are decidedly tender and are mostly grown in hothouses. They are the best for forcing into bloom for a winter display. They cannot be grown outside anywhere in Britain; but in warm, hot climates, especially along the coast of the Gulf of Mexico, they flourish luxuriantly and are a glorious sight. One of the finest collections is at the Bellingrath Gardens near Mobile, Alabama.

But we have a vast number of hardy kinds to choose from for our own gardens; those with deep glowing brilliant colours are specially recommended for people who have only a small garden.

# CHAPTER TWO

## *Evergreens that are Easy to Grow*

RHODODENDRONS are no doubt the best of the flowering evergreens that we can grow – with the exception perhaps of Camellias; and they require more care and attention than many other evergreen shrubs and trees. Soil conditions must be right. Adequate preparation is necessary – deep digging; trenching on poor ground; adding peat or leafmould are jobs which often have to be done. But there are evergreens which don't give any trouble at all when grown in the average garden, the garden, that is, where the soil has been cultivated for some years.

Virgin soil (in a new garden) may or may not be good. It needs enriching with plenty of organic manure if it's shallow and sandy; and certainly it will have to be cleared of weeds and rubbish before anything can be planted.

Yet there is an evergreen shrub which will succeed even in the poorest soils, or in full sun, or deep shade, and exposed places – high or low. That remarkable shrub is *Mahonia aquifolium* (having 'pointed' – Holly-like leaves), formerly known as *Berberis aquifolium*, and called the Holly-leaf Berberis. It is an excellent choice for planting in a new garden, where the soil is especially poor and starved.

It is a perfect weed smotherer, provided it is kept down to about 18 inches by pruning it back regularly every year. If you leave it unpruned, it will go up to a height of 5 feet or more and make an open, straggling shrub which in shape, at least, is not particularly attractive. (You can incidentally train it into a standard, by leaving a single stem and cutting out all side shoots and suckers from the base as they appear. In time the stem will become thick and trunk-like.)

The leaves are roughly Holly-shaped and spiny and turn a charming bronzy-red in autumn and winter (some on slightly damaged or broken branches, I've noticed, turn vivid scarlet).

The flowers are singularly beautiful; they are a bright lemon-yellow and are carried in erect racemes or clusters about 3 inches long, sometimes in full bloom very early in the year – February – but usually in March and April. In autumn the stems are crowded with clusters of blue-black berries, which are conspicuous against the glossy green foliage and persist till the frosts come.

If you leave them where they drop – even on a gravel path – they will germinate and make sturdy little seedlings the following year. Propagation by seeds (berries) is easy and costs nothing; and you can increase your stock a hundredfold, if you wish. Another method is by cuttings; and unflowered shoots strike easily out of doors: choose pieces about 6 inches long and insert them in sandy leafy soil in a shady spot.

You can fill a whole border with this amazing plant (at Kew you will see long borders of it – and no weeds!); you can plant it all over your garden, if you wish; it doesn't mind drought and dry soils. You can have a hedge of it, a low one, however, if you want it neat and dense. Plant two rows, the shrubs 18 inches apart and the rows 2 feet apart.

I have interplanted a group with the winter-blooming *Jasmine nudiflorum*, the well-known yellow-flowered climber which is mostly grown (and is really best) on walls. Its long thin stems covered with star-shaped yellow flowers in winter fall across the bronze-red foliage of the shrubs and give a bright bit of colour through the grey months of the year.

Owners of large estates use the shrub for game-coverts, since it thrives and grows well in deep shade among any kinds of trees, deciduous or evergreen. The only place where it fails is on water-logged ground.

We used to be able to buy the shrub quite cheaply by the hundred or the thousand; but now (1967) a single specimen costs 7*s*. 6*d*. or more. However, you can raise your own by seeds. It is everybody's plant. It heads my list of easy-to-grow evergreens. Others, almost as accommodating, belong to the Berberis family.

Mahonia and Berberis are closely related to one another and at one time both were described under the genus *Berberis*.

Mahonias are easily distinguished from the Berberis by their compound leaves (see Fig. 1, showing a leaf, pinnate, of *Mahonia aquifolium*), and spineless stems. Furthermore, they

5. *Magnolia Grandiflora*—A magnificent evergreen tree.

6. Camellia Var. J. C. Williams are of the loveliest of garden camellias.

7. *Senecio Laxifolius*, a favourite silver-grey evergreen.

8. Massed low-growing heathers will keep the weeds down.

are all evergreens, whereas may of the Berberis are deciduous.

Before we choose any more of the 'easy' Mahonias, let us look at some of the Berberis – those that are almost as tough and as attractive as *M. aquifolium.*

*Fig.* 1. Showing a leaf pinnate of *Mahonia aquifolium*

*Berberis X stenophylla* (with narrow leaves) is one of them. It is a hybrid (*B. darwinii X B. empetrifolia*) and grew first in a nursery near Sheffield in 1860. Like *Mahonia aquifolium*, it will flourish in practically any garden; it is not fastidious as to soil; it should however be started off in some good loam; but once established, it needs no further attention apart from pruning it back when it gets too big for the place where you've planted it (ultimately it makes a big bush 10 feet high and 10 or 12 feet through).

It makes a fine specimen shrub for a lawn; it does well on slopes, and is often used, like *Mahonia aquifolium*, for covering them and keeping the weeds down. As a hedge it is magnificent and soon forms an impenetrable mass of spiny arching stems wreathed in April and May with tiny rich golden-yellow flowers. The leaves, narrow, are a fresh green, hard and spine-tipped.

The plant is easily propagated by cuttings; these are inserted in sandy soil (or in pure sand) under a cloche during the summer. But plants raised from seed are reversions, having mostly the character of *B. darwinii.*

*B. darwinii* (named in honour of Charles Darwin, the eminent naturalist and scientist); it needs ordinary loamy soil and does best sheltered from cold north and east winds during its early years, but apart from that, is no trouble. It has been described as one of the loveliest of all evergreen shrubs; and the colour of the flowers is the most striking of all the Berberis flowers – a vivid golden orange, practically the same colour as the fruit itself. The flowers come in small drooping clusters and bloom in April. The leaves are small and a dark glossy green and spiny.

A specimen shrub after many years' growth will probably reach a height of 12 feet and measure twice that through. It is a favourite plant for hedging and for screens, and most attractive in autumn when it bears clusters of pea-sized, plum-coloured fruits.

Another good screening Berberis is the species *B. julianiae.* It is a dense evergreen, with small spiny-toothed leaves in clusters, and small yellow flowers. It will grow in any garden and in practically any soil. Tall specimens may be seen in gardens around London, measuring 8 feet tall and more than that in diameter.

And another good hedging Berberis is *B. gagnepainii* (named in honour of Father Gagnepain of the *Muséum National of Paris.* Botanist. Born 1868). It was introduced by Wilson from Szechwan, China in 1904. A shrub, spiny all over – one has to be careful when pruning it (use gloves). The flowers are bright yellow, small and come in clusters; they bloom in late May and are lovely against the dark green narrowish leaves.

The flowers of many of the Berberis are small and come in clusters; those of *B. darwinii* are conspicuous because of their brilliant orange colour. Those of *B. candidula* stand out well, being carried singly on slender stalks and measuring nearly ¾-inch across. They are an attractive bright yellow. The leaves, a shining green above and a vivid whitish colour beneath are an excellent foil. *B. candidula* (shining, dazzling) is a fine choice for small gardens, forming as it does, a roundish, or dome-shaped shrub about 3 feet high. It's a cheerful sight in winter and as it is so slow in growth, it makes a good plant for a rockery. An excellent background for any of the brilliantly-coloured spring Alpines.

One can learn much from other people's successes and failures. Several gardeners living in different parts of the country have sent me lists of evergreen Berberis that they considered the most ornamental and the most suitable for growing anywhere. These shrubs succeed in any soil, limy or leafy or sandy and in any situations; though *Berberis japonica* and its varieties, and *B. pinnata* want a little more care and attention than the others.

These two Berberis are now described under the genus *Mahonia* and will be found in catalogues under that name.

First, three of the true Berberis:—

*B. hookeri*, a dense evergreen shrub up to 5 feet tall; leaves glaucous (green above, white beneath); and the flowers, small, pale yellow with reddish sepals. (The plant is named in honour of Sir W. J. Hooker, 1785–1865, Director of Kew; or of his son Sir Joseph D. Hooker, 1817–1911, traveller in the Himalaya, who succeeded is father as Director of Kew.)

The variety: VIRIDIS (green) has leaves coloured bright green beneath. Both shrubs are ideal for a limited space, since they retain their dwarf character without any pruning.

*B. verruculosa* (somewhat verrucose: covered with wart-like excrescences). Familiarly known as the Warted Barberry: the branches are covered with tiny wart-like growths. The leaves, of a leathery texture, are glaucous, and the flowers, golden-yellow, bloom in May. The shrub has attractive blue-black berries in autumn. Another low-growing compact evergreen.

The Mahonias were:—

*Mahonia japonica* (of Japan). A tall shrub with delightfully fragrant flowers which open in February (the scent is reminiscent of Lily-of-the-Valley). They are a lemon-yellow colour and come in great abundance in erect racemes, 6 to 9 inches long, and are one of the joys of the garden in winter. They don't seem to mind frost. The foliage is particularly handsome and striking – it has in fact an exotic look about it – the leaflets are dark green, hard and stiff, and number 7 to 13 on each long, leaf-stalk. As in all the *Mahonia*, the *leaves* are pinnate (feather-like in arrangement) or compound, the *leaflets* coming on each side of the petiole or leaf-stalk. (See Fig. 1.)

The actual length of the compound leaf is from 1 to 1½-feet long, the leaflets varying from 2 to 5 inches in length. The purple berries are ½-inch long and oblong in shape.

*M. bealei* (named in honour of Thomas Chay Beale, who helped Robert Fortune in his collecting); it is sometimes listed as a variety of *M. japonica*. It is more striking even than that shrub, its leaflets are larger (8 inches long and often 6 inches wide); its flowers finer. Both grow to a good height: often 10 feet or more. One gardener who had these two Berberis at the top of his list, stated that both shrubs when first planted should have overhead protection during the winter, if it is very severe. There is usually a sheltered spot in most gardens; and such magnificent shrubs as these certainly deserve it.

*M. pinnata* (pinnate leaves). It has been described as a variety of the popular *M. aquifolium* (page 31); but it differs from that shrub in several ways: it grows much taller as a rule; it has been known to reach a height of 12 feet in south-west Ireland, and its evergreen leaves are a dull grey-green and are composed of as many as 13 leaflets to each leaf. The rich yellow flowers carried in erect racemes appear on the stems as well as at the top of the shrub. They are wonderfully fragrant and valuable for cutting for indoors.

The smallest of these Mahonias cost about 15*s*. 6*d*. each.

*Laurel* and *Privet* sound the most uninteresting of all evergreens; yet there are at least two Privets which are fine garden shrubs and very ornamental: one is *Ligustrum lucidum*, sometimes a tree up to 30 feet high; the other, *L. delavayanum*, a small-leaved spreading shrub, usually not more than 6 feet tall. These

Privets display their beauty to best advantage when grown as specimen shrubs.

*L. lucidum* (clear, shining) makes a tall, handsome tree up to about 30 feet or more. (In its habitat Hupeh, China, it has been found 60 feet tall.) The leaves are ovalish in shape, 3 to 6 inches long; and the flowers, white, come in erect terminal panicles 6 to 8 inches long. These are very conspicuous during the early autumn and welcome during a time when there is a scarcity of flowers in the garden.

The variety TRICOLOR is not so hardy, but very striking in the colour of its foliage; the leaves have a broad band of white; and when young, this is a pretty pink colour.

*L. delavayanum* (named in honour of l'Abbé Jean M. Delavay, 1834–95, who collected many plants in West China), sometimes called *L. pratti*. It is a native of Yunnan, China, and was raised in France by a nurseryman from seed sent to him by the Abbé Delavay in 1890. The dark, shining green leaves are smaller than those of the common Privet; the flowers white; the berries black. It is a fine Privet for a small garden, making a flat-branching, spreading shrub up to about 6 feet high. As the plant matures, it becomes more rounded. In gardens along the south coast I have seen some specimens 10 feet or more in height.

The common Privet, *L. vulgare* (common) is only partially evergreen, and an inferior garden plant; in fact I can't think of any place where it could be grown effectively – perhaps it is best for filling up places where nothing else would grow. It is considered to be a native of this country and is found wild in our hedgerows. I advise gardeners to choose other species for hedging, however, if they want Privet. The Oval-leaved Privet (*L. ovalifolium*) is a much superior plant. The popular Golden Privet, a favourite hedging plant, is a variety called AUREUM of the oval-leaf species.

Privet thrives in any soil, but it won't grow well in very stony ground; like every plant, it should be given a good start off.

Plants are easily raised by cuttings inserted in sandy soil in a shady spot out of doors. This is the cheapest way of obtaining a good stock for hedges.

The common Laurel is *Prunus laurocerasus* (Laurel-Cherry) and is a more handsome foliage-shrub or tree than any of the Privets. It comes in for more criticism perhaps than any other evergreen we grow, yet it has many virtues. Its dark, shining green leaves are among the most attractive of all evergreen leaves; it makes a magnificent tall shrub or tree if left unpruned – a fine specimen tree 20 feet or more tall, which is an excellent wind-break. It flourishes in any ordinary soil, it doesn't even mind dry soils and revels in windy exposed places. Like *Mahonia aquifolium*, it thrives in woodland, where it makes a good dense undergrowth.

On the other hand, it quickly impoverishes the soil where it grows, depriving all other plants near it of the sustenance they need. It has very little floral beauty: the flowers, a dull white, come in small terminal racemes and are scarcely noticeable; and it is sometimes damaged by frost during a severe winter and is not so hardy as *P. lusitanica* (the Portugal Laurel).

Both species are used for hedging and screening; but unless one can have a double row of the shrubs, the result will be a rather thin open hedge. Pruning and shaping the plants is a lengthy job, since the growths should be cut back with a pair of secateurs, not with shears, which easily mutilate the leaves. (I'm afraid I always use shears, since clipping is much quicker than systematic pruning.)

There are several good varieties of the common Laurel; two of the best are CAUCASICA, which has dark green, rather narrow leaves; and SCHIPKAENSIS, the hardiest of all the Laurels; it survives severe frosts, snow, winds and storms. Its leaves are narrow, usually about 4 inches long and 1½ inches wide. These two are probably the most useful for the average garden.

The plant is a native of E. Europe and Asia Minor and was introduced into Britain at the beginning of the 17th century.

*P. lusitanica* (Portuguese) is a native of Spain and was introduced into England round about the same time as the common Laurel. As already mentioned, it is somewhat hardier than the common sort, provided it grows in well-drained, sandy soils (start it off in some good loam).

It vies in beauty of flowers and fruits with any of the other numerous varieties; the flowers come in long, slender racemes in June and are hawthorn-scented and the fruits which follow are large and a dark reddish-purple. The shrub is seen at its best when left unpruned and grown as a single specimen.

Var. AZORICA is the largest-leaved form (in hot climates it goes up to a height of 60 feet or more). It received a F.C.C. in 1896.

*Cotoneaster* and *Pyracantha* are two families of evergreen shrubs which are very easy to grow.

*Cotoneaster* (pronounced with the accent on the second syllable: co-*to*-ne-as-ter) will grow and flourish in any soil that isn't waterlogged or boggy, and they settle down well in the poorest soils. They are all very hardy, and as garden shrubs their greatest attraction is their bright coloured berries. Their flowers are small and by no means showy. (Mention Cotoneaster to a gardener and he'll immediately think of berries, not flowers.)

There is a good number of evergreen species and varieties; those I recommend do not take up a great deal of room. I think most of them can be accommodated in the average-sized border; and several are suitable for the rockery.

One of these is *C. congesta* (congested; arranged very closely together: referring to the branches); the short branches which form mound-like masses of green, are covered in autumn with bright red berries measuring ¼ inch across. It seldom goes above a height of 2 feet and gives a touch of colour to the rock-garden late in the year – and how much we appreciate it! Several grouped in a semi-shady border make a perfect dull green background for the dwarf Japanese Azaleas described in the preceding chapter.

*C. microphylla* (small leaves); it has small glossy green leaves (grey and woolly beneath) and scarlet berries. I have seen the shrub used for covering a sunny slope – perhaps a dozen plants altogether and very attractive in autumn, the berries remarkably showy against the deep glossy green foliage. The variety COCHLEATA is more compact and more striking in fruit: the berries, a deep scarlet colour, are borne freely in October. The shrub received an A.M. in 1931. (Beautiful fruiting sprays were exhibited at the R.H.S. Show at the beginning of October of that year.)

There are taller kinds, which make fine specimen shrubs for lawns. *C. salicifolia* (with willow-like leaves) and its varieties are good shrubs for this purpose. They carry heavy crops of berries in autumn and are tall graceful plants.

Var. FLOCCOSA has leathery narrow leaves and bright red fruits; and Var. RUGOSA has larger leaves and fruit than FLOCCOSA and is a coarser-looking, more vigorous plant. Both varieties were discovered by the collector Wilson in Western

China, who described them as some of the most beautiful of all berrying shrubs for the garden.

*C. pannosa* (like coarse cloth in texture; woolly); this is another Cotoneaster which makes a fine specimen shrub. It goes up to a height of 10 feet or more, with slender arching branches covered with small oval leaves, dull green above and white and woolly beneath; and red fruits in October.

I prefer *C. turbinata* (top-shaped – the fruits), perhaps because I know it better; it is about the same height as *C. pannosa* and is of the same graceful habit and it grows quickly. Its leaves are about 2 inches long and 1 inch wide, dark green above and white beneath. The fruits are deep red in October and pear-shaped (top-shaped). Both species are natives of China.

These berrying Cotoneasters are seen to best advantage when they are massed in a large bed, one kind only being used. The berries are obviously more conspicuous then. You need plenty of room, of course – you get the most striking effects when you grow a plant in a mass.

In a small garden, however, this isn't possible. All we can do is to grow something else with a plant to enhance its beauty. With the Cotoneasters we could use some autumn-tinting shrub as a background-piece – one of the lovely yellow-coloured Maples, for instance. The scarlet ones would naturally eclipse the beauty of the red fruits. Autumn Crocuses that bloom in October and November, is another suggestion. These should be massed round the shrub or planted in drifts in front of it. *Crocus kotschyanus* (rosy-lilac) blooms at the end of September. *C. speciosus var AITCHISONII* (pale lilac) and *C. salzmannii* (lilac), bloom at the beginning of October; and *C. pulchellus* (bluish-lilac) usually begins to open its flowers in November. Try any of these with, say, *Cotoneaster turbinata.*

*Pyracantha*, related to *Cotoneaster*, are more often than not grown against a wall and scarcely need any companion plants – the grey stone or the red brick affords sufficient contrast.

'Firethorns' is the popular name of these evergreens; the colour of the berries is mostly a fiery-red and the branches are thorny. On a wall the plants often attain a height of 15 feet or much more, depending on the climate. But when grown in the open garden as bushes, they are not so tall.

Practically any soil suits them, though a light loam is better than a heavy clay.

The favourite and possibly the most successful species is *P. coccinea* (scarlet), a European plant, known by its French name *Buisson* (bush) *Ardent* (burning); it was introduced into this country at the beginning of the 17th century. Its leaves are oval shaped, dark glossy green above, and paler beneath. The flowers, small and insignificant like those of the *Cotoneaster*, are white and open in June. The fiery-red berries stand out remarkably against the green foliage and are a magnificent sight through the autumn and winter months. (Unfortunately birds devour them.) Some people net the shrubs to keep the birds off; but I've found that they usually tire of them after one good feed.

The variety LALANDII is a bigger, finer shrub, with large berries of an enchanting deep orange-red colour.

*P. angustifolia* (narrow leaves). One of the great virtues of this plant is that the orange-yellow berries last an astonishingly long time, often till the spring – long after those of *P. coccinea* have fallen. It is a large shrub, usually reaching a height of 12 feet and of a bushy, spreading habit. The leaves are an attractive dark green colour and covered with grey felt beneath. A more tender plant than the common species, described above. It is a native of China and was first grown in Britain at Kew Botanic Gardens in 1899.

*P. rogersiana* (named in honour of Mr. Coltman-Rogers of Radnorshire, who first exhibited the plant at one of the Royal Horticultural Society's Shows in 1913); it is described by many gardeners as the best of all the *Pyracantha*, both as a specimen shrub and as a wall-plant. The berries are a reddish-orange colour – very brilliant – and the leaves exceptionally small: about 1 inch long and ½ inch wide. The flowers (white) come in small panicles in June; but, as with all the Pyracantha flowers, they are not much to look at.

*Pyracantha* grown against a wall must have their side shoots trained in the direction required; and the foreright (frontal) shoots must be cut back to keep the plants neat and compact.

Some years ago in a garden on the south coast I saw the species *P. rogersiana* used for a hedge and covered with berries in late autumn. The hedge was about 6 feet high and was clipped back every year; apparently hard clipping does no harm.

The great drawback to planting such a hedge is the expensiveness of the plants – most of them cost about 13*s*. each. Fortunately Pyracantha can be propagated both by seeds and by cuttings. Set the cuttings (select firm, leafy twigs) in sandy soil in a shady frame; the best time is the end of August.

In the same district were hedges of the glossy-leaved evergreen *Euonymus japonica*. It isn't a plant everybody likes, yet it seems to be a favourite for hedges – especially in the south, where it actually grows best. North of London it often succumbs to frost. It does well enough here, in South Bucks., but its leaves are nearly always attacked and disfigured by swarms of caterpillars which spin thick ugly cobwebs over the plants and feed on the leaves. Spraying with one of the insecticides is necessary every spring to get rid of the pests.

The species is a native of Japan, where it grows up to a height of 30 feet or more, making a tree of densely leafy habit.

There are many varieties, mostly variegated, such as Var. ALBA-MARGINATA, with leaves margined with white; Var. MICROPHYLLA VARIEGATA: leaves margined with silver.

*E. radicans* (having rooting stems); this is a creeping evergreen, used for a ground cover or for training up walls; grown in the latter way, it will reach a height of 20 feet or more. The leaves are a pleasing dark green colour, smooth, and ovalish in shape, about 1 inch long.

In some countries where the Ivy is not hardy, *E. radicans* is used instead of that plant for training up walls of houses, and it is also clipped down small for an edging like Box. It resembles Ivy in that when it reaches the adult, flowering stage, its shoots become erect and bushy; and, like the Ivy, it will flourish in deep shade. The leaves of these bushy forms are larger: and the plants when pruned back regularly make useful evergreen shrubs – Ivy and its different forms are described and discussed in Chapter 9, page 174. *E. radicans*, like *E. japonica*, is also a native of Japan, and has produced several charming variegated forms. Var. ROSEO-MARGINATA has pinkish markings, and I think the most attractive.

These Euonymus will grow in any ordinary soil and they do extremely well in chalky, limy ground.

I am mentioning *Cistus X purpureus* here among the easy-to-grow evergreens because it was described to me recently by a gardener as being the loveliest of all flowering evergreen shrubs and one that would grow in any poor soil. This is only partly true; there is a serious omission in the description. And that is that the plant is not truly hardy. It succeeds only in warm maritime districts such as Cornwall and Devon.

The finest specimens will be found on dry, sandy slopes facing the Mediterranean. The open flowers (like crinkled silk) are purplish-pink, with a red blotch at the base of each petal, and practically cover the shrub – the narrow dull green leaves are visible only after the flowers have fallen – usually late in the evening. It is regarded as the best of all the Cistus and is actually one of the most beautiful of evergreen shrubs. Unfortunately there are few gardens in this country where it will live very long. It is described in the Chapter dealing with the Rock-rose family (page 146).

The Periwinkles, *Vinca major* and *V. minor* flourish in sun or shade and in any soil. They flower more profusely in sun and make a good undergrowth for shrubs like the Brooms. The blue of the Periwinkles looks well beneath the yellow of these shrubs.

*V. major* (large) blooms from May to September and carries its flowers on upright stems about 18 inches high; its long trailing stems are barren, but produce dark glossy green leaves which are attractive all through the year. Plenty of new young plants can be obtained from the stems which root where they touch the ground.

*V. minor* (little, small) is a dwarf, trailing plant, the stems rarely more than 6 inches long. It is easily distinguished from the other species by the smaller flowers and leaves – it is smaller in all its parts.

There are some very charming varieties, viz. Var. ALBA, with white flowers; Var. PLENA, with double flowers; Var. PUNICEA, purple. But the type plant, with its 'Periwinkle blue' flowers I consider the best.

Both species come from Southern Europe, and they are found growing wild in Britain but are probably escapes from cultivation. As the Periwinkle does not perfect its seed here, it is doubtful whether they are natives.

Finally, the popular Laurustinus (*Viburnum tinus*), a valuable easy-to-grow evergreen for screening. It also makes a good hedge, but doesn't flower freely when clipped every season. As a flowering hedge (left unpruned), it is rather untidy and in time grows very wide, with long straggling shoots. This is how

*Fig.* 2. Flatish clusters—Cymes—of Laurustinus flowers

I like to see it and it is all right in a large garden; but for boundary hedges the plant is usually clipped to make the growth fairly uniform. And it seems to do better when planted in a mass.

Laurustinus thrives in any ordinary soil, provided it is of a reasonably good depth and well drained; and in sun or shade. In shady, sheltered places it grows taller but does not bloom so freely. Around London the plant can be damaged by frost during a severe winter; but is not usually killed; in my garden in South Bucks., parts of the shrubs (20-year old plants, now 10 to 12 feet high) were damaged by frost two years ago. The leaves turned brown after some months and died, and later some of the stems died back. But strong new shoots have sprung up from round the base, and new growths have also developed on the lower branches. There are still one or two gaps in some of the shrubs, but most of them are again thick with fresh green foliage from top to bottom.

One of the beauties of this excellent evergreen is that no main stem or trunk, or branches can be seen through the mass of foliage. No shrub could be better for screening in the average garden; but I wouldn't recommend it for cold northern gardens – though many gardeners do.

The flowers come in flattish clusters (cymes) – see Fig. 2, page 44. They are about 4 inches across, pinkish in the bud and turn white as they develop. They begin to open about October and, depending on the weather, bloom freely till April. The leaves are a delightful glossy green, pale beneath; and the berries which often remain on the branches till the flowers come again are blue-black in colour.

*V. tinus* has produced several attractive varieties – two decidedly on the tender side.

Var. LUCIDUM (clear, shining); this is looser in habit than the type plant; and the leaves and flowers are larger, the former often 4 inches long and 2 inches wide, and a striking polished green. It does well in gardens along the south-west coast; but is a failure in districts around London.

Var. HIRTUM (hairy); the shoots, stalks and the base of the leaves are covered with hairs, the leaves slightly thicker in texture. It is often grown in a cool greenhouse, the winter flowers being much in demand by florists.

Var. PURPUREUM is a charming hardy variety with dark green leaves, which are tinged purple when young.

Var. VARIEGATUM has variegated leaves, part of the leaf, sometimes all one side, a golden-yellow.

Like the trailing stems of the Vincas, the lower stems of the

*Fig.* 3. Stem of Laurustinus rooting in the ground

Laurustinus trail on the ground and often root there; this is the easiest way of propagating the shrub. See Fig. 3. And all the Laurustinus are easily increased by cuttings put in a frame; if bottom heat can be given, they root much more quickly.

## CHAPTER THREE

# *Evergreen Trees*

TREES vary considerably in size. There are the giants of our woods and forests, such as Oak, Beech, Elm; and much bigger than these are the Redwoods of California. In Britain Redwoods don't grow anywhere near as big but we have many Firs (*Abies grandis*), for instance, which are well over a hundred feet tall.

There are many smaller kinds; most of our ornamental trees are not more than 20 or 30 feet in height; the popular flowering Almond (*Prunus communis*) is a moderate-sized tree. Our standard fruit trees are about the same size. (A *Standard* is a single stem or trunk.) And a small garden can usually accommodate one or two. Some people prefer an apple and a pear tree, probably because these fruits keep reasonably well. Others plant ornamentals, such as the *Prunus*. Most of the loveliest are deciduous, and those trees gardeners prize are often precocious, the blossom appearing before the leaves.

What sort of evergreen trees can we grow? There are not many; and none is as beautiful in flower as the deciduous kinds. The exceptions are the tall Rhododendrons and some of the Camellias, growing either in their habitats or under climatic conditions similar to those they enjoy in nature. *Rhododendron arboreum* (tree-like) grows to tree-size in parts of Cornwall; and I have seen varieties of *Camellia japonica* as tall as trees, with thick trunks, growing at Ascona (in Italian Switzerland) on the shores of Lake Maggiore.

For a magnificent and lasting show of blossom, the Camellias are unsurpassed; but they don't reach tree-size in Britain.

One of our most attractive evergreen trees is *Arbutus unedo* (literally: 'I eat one'), known as the 'Strawberry Tree' in England; and in Southern Ireland (where it grows wild and the finest specimens are found), the 'Killarney Strawberry Tree'. 'Strawberry' refers to the fruit this *Arbutus* bears when the flowers perish. It is a rounded drupe, orange-red in colour and full of seeds. Not a dessert fruit, in fact it's not at all palatable, but it is extremely decorative on the tree, where it ripens during the autumn of the second year; the pinkish-white flowers are likewise at their best (October to December), and the effect of the orange-red fruits and flowers is delightful at this time of the year.

The dark, shining green leaves afford an excellent contrast and make a fine background to the pink-and-white and orange-red colours. The leaves are from 2 to 4 inches long and ½ inch to 2 inches wide.

This *Arbutus* is a native of the Mediterranean regions and of South-West Ireland, where magnificent trees up to 40 feet will be seen either in gardens or growing wild in the warm-west districts on the Atlantic seaboard.

In England it is smaller and on ordinary soils often shrub-like (good specimens however may be seen in many parts of the country). It prefers deep moist acid loam or peat (which it gets in Killarney), but will thrive and flourish on lime-stone formations and will actually tolerate a certain amount of lime in the soil.

I would hesitate to grow it in my own garden, I think; yet as I say, many good specimens can be found in inland gardens – and as far north as Yorkshire. The finest I have seen so far (outside Killarney), which made wide-topped trees, grew in southern maritime districts and faced the gales that blew in from the sea.

The best time for planting Arbutus is in late September, and only the smallest specimens should be grown, since the shrub transplants badly – large specimens more often than not collapse after they are shifted. The normal way of raising *Arbutus* is by seeds – named varieties are grafted on seedlings of *A. unedo*.

Those who want to try one of the varieties of the 'Strawberry Tree' should get Var. RUBRA (red); the flowers, rich reddish-pink, are more striking than those of the type plant. This variety was given an A.M. in 1925. A good specimen can be bought for about 30*s*.

The most magnificent of all the *Arbutus* is the species *A. menziesii* (probably in honour of Archibald Menzies, 1754–1842, botanist and naval surgeon). It is known as the Madrona, a noble evergreen tree up to 100 feet tall in its native California;

its trunk is often 6 feet thick and as the bark peels away, it reveals its beautiful shining cinnamon colour. The branches are similarly coloured – looking as though they had been polished. (The Spanish for Arbutus is *Madroño*; the word also means a round tassel.)

In Britain the tree seldom goes above 30 feet or so; at Kew there is a fairish specimen which is perfectly hardy – the species does better in the warmer south than in the north and according to many gardeners must have a rich moist loam. This no doubt is true of newly-planted young trees which, like many rare plants, want a specially good start off.

But people who have seen the Madrona growing in the wild in California tell me it flourishes luxuriantly in dry parched hot places, often among the rocks.

The trees were of course planted by Nature, from seed, and through the course of years (fed by rich soil washed down to them by torrential rains) have grown into marvellously strong healthy specimens. They are a feature of the valleys of Northern California; the polished red trunks, shining green leaves, and above, the erect panicles of flowers and orange fruits, are visible for miles, and beautiful in the fading light of a spring afternoon. They are as much a spectacle as the giant Cactus plants which stand up like egregious monuments in the vast desert regions of Arizona.

The noble Madrona is seldom seen in our gardens; venturesome gardeners will doubtless give it a trial. Young plants can be obtained from our leading shrub nurseries and cost about 30*s*. each. A reasonably protected site should be found for this *Arbutus*.

Another spectacular evergreen tree is the Monkey Puzzle (*Araucaria araucana*), which is more curious than beautiful and, to many people, something of an oddity. (It is a conifer; see Chapter 7 for a description of some of these most useful evergreen cone-bearing trees). We see the Monkey Puzzle in many gardens, and the astonishing thing is that they are found in so many small or moderate-sized gardens. It seems that small plants, about 9 inches high, could be bought very cheaply from nurseries in early Victorian times, and perhaps the strange, exotic appearance of the plant (introduced in 1795) attracted gardeners in those days. Furthermore, it thrives in ordinary soil – and perhaps most important of all: it was a tree that most people would turn round and look at twice! I doubt very much whether it is grown today – Hillier lists it, but no price is given.

The Monkey Puzzle is completely hardy. It must be planted as an isolated specimen, for there is nothing suitable to go with it. (The epithet *araucana* is the name of the Indian race inhabiting the region of S. Chile where the tree was first found.)

Several of the evergreen trees recommended by growers and nurseries are not hardy enough for every district in this country. Two or three in fact are quite tender: *Acacia dealbata* (the Silver Wattle), for instance, is suitable only for the warmest maritime regions, and even there is sometimes cut to the ground during the winter; it is the well known Mimosa, with yellow fluffy very fragrant flowers and grey-green fern-like foliage, which we get from the French Riviera at the beginning of the year. I've known shrub enthusiasts try to grow it near London; but here it will survive only when planted in a cool greenhouse, as it does at Kew. An attempt was made many years ago to grow it in the sheltered, walled garden of Brampton House, Marlow-on-Thames. The owner, Mrs. Olga Kann, showed it me soon after she had planted it. The most protected spot against a south wall had been chosen for it, and it was covered completely by suitable protective material during frosty weather; but the plant didn't live very long.

There are good specimens to be found in gardens along the coasts of Hampshire, and of course farther south, in the Scilly Isles, and the south-west districts of Ireland.

This *Acacia* is a native of parts of Australia, and of Tasmania, from which country it was introduced into Britain in 1820. In Nature it will sometimes reach a height of a 100 feet, with a trunk 10 feet or more in girth; but in gardens it usually makes a moderate-sized tree about 30 feet tall. Those who think they can grow it, should give it an open peaty or loamy soil in good heart.

Another Australian evergreen tree is the *Eucalyptus*. There are several species, nearly all of them listed in catalogues as 'only hardy in the mildest localities': for most of us, then, they aren't much good.

The hardiest is *E. gunnii* (named in honour of R. C. Gunn

1808–81, of Tasmania). Tall specimens may be seen in inland gardens in Britain: at Kew the tree is about 40 feet high; and there is a taller, finer tree which I have seen in the grounds of Powerscourt, near Dublin.

The great attraction of the Eucalyptus is their picturesque, glaucous-green or glaucous-blue foliage, and also the coloured bark of the trunks. (The plural *Eucalypts*, by the way, appears in some botanical works, and *Eucalypti* in others.) The trees have little if any floral beauty; and in Britain *E. gunnii* (known as the Cider Tree) is the wisest choice.

If a young plant is obtained, and well protected for a few years during severe winters, it will in all probability grow into a good strong specimen, having formed a stout woody base.

Give it a deep moist loam and a position near a warm wall, if you can.

The Eucalypts are easily raised from seed (obtainable from any seedsman); and the tender species *E. cordata* (heart-shaped leaves) can be raised by the hundred; this is a striking glaucous-white foliage-plant used solely in England, I believe, for adorning formal flower-beds during the summer months.

The smell of the oil in the leaves is liked by many people; it is at once perceptible when the leaves are bruised in the fingers.

Yet another evergreen tree recommended by some, but regarded as a doubtful hardy by most, is the so-called Californian Laurel, *Umbellularia californica* (of California), a tree from 80–100 feet tall in its native habitat of California and Oregon. It is known as the 'Spice Bush' on account of the pungent smell of the leaves when crushed.

The leaves are dark green and glossy, the largest about 5 inches long and 2 inches wide. The small, greenish flowers are insignificant; the fruit pea-shaped and purplish when ripe.

The species, the only one known, was introduced into England in 1829; a good specimen grows at Kew and is injured there only by severe frosts. It wants a deep, moist loam and is unsuitable for shallow, chalky soils.

Most nurseries have the plant and it costs about a guinea.

The Bay Tree (*Laurus nobilis*) is known to most people, principally for its aromatic leaves, which are used in cookery: a bay-leaf is one of the ingredients of the *Bouquet-garni* used for flavouring soups, sauces, etc. Cooks know the tree as well as gardeners do. (The leaves are kept till they are dried and then stored in air-tight containers.) One would imagine the tree would be seen often in gardens. In the old walled-gardens of the past, when the vegetable and fruit plot was enclosed by 10-feet walls, the Bay was fairly common and usually planted by the south wall, and prospered there, only being damaged during exceptionally severe weather. The leaves are occasionally browned by frosts in the open garden, but the tree seldom succumbs to cold in this country.

The Bay came to us from the Mediterranean region in the 16th century and, like other plants indigenous to those parts, flourishes most luxuriantly in our warm seaside gardens – the finest specimens of Cistus (Rock Roses) and Lavender (both from the Mediterranean) grow in our southern counties.

The Bay Tree in this district, 30 miles from London, is more of a tall bush than a tree; there is an oldish specimen at Woburn House, near High Wycombe, and when I saw it last it was about 15 feet tall, a dense healthy tall shrub that had thrown out one or two deeply-rooted suckers from the base.

The leaves, oval in shape, are about 4 inches long, and of a dark glossy green colour. Their pleasant smell is quickly noticeable on a warm, sunny day.

The shrub is a favourite one for clipping into different shapes. You can see them in small wooden tubs at many of the leading West End Stores; and these topiary trees or shrubs are enormously expensive. You can buy a small natural specimen from a shrub nursery for about 15*s*.

The Bay leaf was the leaf chosen by the ancients to make wreaths and crowns for heroes during victory celebrations: it is called by us the Laurel – 'crowned with Laurels'; but the 'Laurel' of those times was the *Laurus nobilis*.

There is a singularly attractive variety with much narrower leaves, called Var. ANGUSTIFOLIA (with small narrow leaves). It is hardier than the other tree.

The Chusan Palm or Fan Palm (*Trachycarpus fortunei*) is recommended by writers on shrubs and trees as suitable for gardens in many parts of the country, and described as an evergreen tree, which will reach a height of 30 feet in favourable districts.

It is less like a tree than the Monkey Puzzle – the familiar name, Chusan or Fan Palm, gives one a clue to what it is like.

It is a gigantic Palm, with huge spiky-looking, much divided (fan-like) leaves, about 2 feet long and 4 feet wide. In my opinion it looks more out of place in the English garden than any other tree or shrub we grow.

Ideally its place is the exotic formal garden, among other semi-tropical plants. However, it is hardy enough for many places; and many gardeners who like novelties will want to grow it. Hillier's nursery, who offer it at about a guinea, state that it is perfectly hardy in the south and the west of the Biritsh Isles, and probably also in most other parts. It likes a rich, loamy soil in good heart, and a top-dressing of well decayed cow manure now and then – apply this in late spring, and not at all the first year; for fresh manure, of this type, keeps the ground cold and damp through the winter; and cold and damp in any form are inimical to the plant's growth and health, as much as a cold north wind is. If you intend growing this fantastic 'tree,' give it the most sheltered spot you can find in your garden. And if you want to create a 'Tropical Corner' in your garden, grow some of the Bamboos along with it. (The different species and varieties of Bamboos are described in Chapter 8, Page 133.)

The plant is named in honour of Robert Fortune, 1812–80 – famous collector in China. The Chusan Palm is a native of Central China.

The evergreen Chestnut, *Castanopsis chrysophylla* (having golden leaves), is hardy enough for most gardens, and thrives in sandy peaty soil of a good depth; it abhors chalky ground. It is, however, an uncommon tree, and in Britain often not much more than a bush; a specimen about 25 feet tall is at Kew and taller specimens are to be found in a few private collections. One of the finest trees in the country grows in the pleasure gardens at Tortworth in Gloucestershire.

The tree's great beauty is in the golden yellow colour of the undersides of the leaves and the young shoots. The plant is in fact called the 'Golden Chestnut.' The leaves, ovalish and pointed, are about 4 inches long; but in the wild, they are much larger and the tree itself is much bigger, often reaching a height of 100 feet or more, with a trunk 6 feet in diameter. The nuts it bears are edible but not as good as those of the Spanish Chestnut.

This *Castanopsis* is a native of Oregon and California and was introduced into Britain about the middle of the 19th century. It is still a rarity in our gardens and so far as I can see not obtainable from any of the nurseries. It is closely related to the Sweet Chestnut (*Castanea*), but it differs in its evergreen foliage – the Sweet Chestnuts are deciduous.

2

The half-a-dozen or so evergreen trees I have mentioned so far, have been either on the tender side and not suitable for every garden in Britain (where trees can be grown) or something of rarities – even oddities. The remaining ones are better known: The Laurel Magnolia (*Magnolia grandiflora*) is the finest as regards foliage and size of flowers (like huge cream-coloured goblets); every town known to me has a specimen growing up the wall of one of the houses. The Evergreen Oaks are the least known, and seen; and a Holly full of bright red berries is probably everybody's favourite evergreen tree.

*Fig.* 4 (*a*). Shows spiny and entire leaves of the Common Holly

The specific name of the Common Holly is *Ilex aquifolium* (pointed, spiny leaves); the plant through the course of centuries of cultivation has produced an enormous number of varieties, many with charming, variegated leaves; some with yellow berries, some with peculiarly-shaped leaves – twisted or contorted, and a number which are quite unattractive and therefore useless as garden plants. Although many of the variegated kinds are grown in our gardens, and especially the entire-leaved (spineless) variety Var. CAMELLIAEFOLIA (see Fig. 4,b), they have never ousted the type plant, which, tree-like or bush-like, or as a hedge, is surely the most attractive red-berried evergreen there is in existence.

*Fig.* 4(*b*). *Var Camelliaefolia* (Camellia-like leaves), a favourite variety of the Common Holly

It will grow in any garden, in any part of the country: in the smoky atmosphere of towns and cities; in high, cold, exposed places, and places on the cold, east coast facing the sea, and in sun or shade. The Holly adapts itself readily to any kind of soil; but new plants should be started off in some good loam.

It is a magnificent tree, up to 80 feet tall: it can be clipped to a shapely bush (it is sometimes used for topiary-work, though is not so suitable as the softer Yew for elaborate shapes), and makes the best of all hedges – dark glossy green all the year, an impenatrable and a gaily coloured object when in fruit.

The leaves on the higher branches of the Holly tree become less spiny, till on the uppermost ones they are smooth (entire) like those of the Camellia. No doubt the spininess of the lower leaves is a natural means of protecting the plant from browsing animals. There are several spineless varieties, as I've already mentioned; but for my part I consider them less attractive than those with spines.

It is practically impossible to transplant a good-sized Holly successfully. Even small specimens must be shifted very carefully, with plenty of soil attached firmly to the roots, and they must be shifted preferably when the roots are still active, which is in May) if not then, the transplanting should be put off till September.

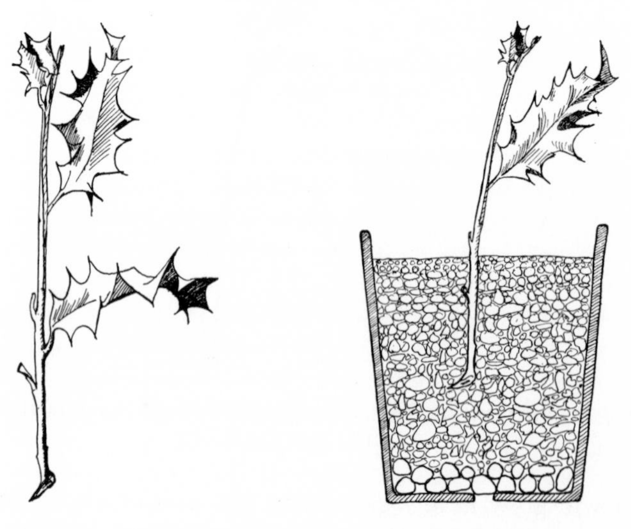

*Fig.* 5. Cuttings of Holly. Use 4-inch shoots with heel attached. Insert in sandy soil

Small plants are sent out from nurseries as a rule, those of the Common Holly costing about 10*s*. 6*d*. per plant; raising them from seed, which is the best way, is a slow job; but you can increase your stock by cuttings, using thin side shoots about 4 inches long, with a heel attached. (See Fig. 5, page 56.) Propagation of the varieties must be effected by this method or by grafting on seedlings of the common plant.

A collector of my acquaintance has a predilection for yellow-berried Hollies and has chosen for his garden the varieties AMBER (originally from Hillier's nursery), which has large bronze-yellow fruits; Var. BACCIFLAVA, with bright yellow berries; and PYRAMIDALIS FRUCTO-LUTEO, an equally beautiful bright yellow-berried variety.

There are dozens more varieties of the Common Holly, the gold and the silver variegated kinds being prized above most of the others by many gardeners. I single out the following for special mention: Var. ARGENTA MARGINATA, the broad-leaved Silver Holly; Var. ARGENTA MARGINATA PENDULA is the weeping form, known as PERRY'S SILVER WEEPING HOLLY, with arching, pendulous branches, a charming specimen tree for the centre of a lawn; Var. FLAVESCENS, leaves suffused with an exquisite canary yellow; Var. GOLDEN QUEEN (a misnomer really, since the plant is a male variety), leaves broadly margined with bright gold; MADAME BRIOT, the centres of the leaves are frequently blotched with green and gold, the edges conspicuously gold in colour; the plant berries freely. There are many others as beautiful as these.

There are male, female (see above) and bi-sexual kinds of the Common Holly; not all of them produce berries freely (some, none at all); hence it is necessary to get those that bear freely; group planting is often resorted to, and ensures berrying of the different varieties.

There is an uncommonly beautiful species called *Ilex latifolia* (broad: referring to the leaves), known as the Tarajo of Japan; it has very thick, burnished green leaves (described by some gardeners as almost as big as those of *Magnolia grandiflora*), the Laurel Magnolia, and carries plenty of red berries. It is no where near as tall in Britain as the Common Holly; in its habitat it reaches a height of 60 feet or more. It is hardy enough at Kew; but is far better growing in our warm maritime districts – some nurseries recommend it for a cold greenhouse.

The collector Sargent regarded it as the most striking large-leaved evergreen tree of Japan. It can be bought at most nurseries and costs about 30*s*.

*Magnolia grandiflora* (large flowers). Popular names for it are the Laurel Magnolia, the Bay Laurel, and the Bull Bay. This *Magnolia* carries larger and more substantial flowers than any other tree we grow in these islands. They are globular, creamy-white in colour, often 10 inches across and delightfully fragrant, smelling of spice. The leaves are ovalish, thick and leathery in texture, from 6 to 10 inches long, and when young are covered beneath with a thick red-brown felt. The leaves are attractive all through the year, and they alone make the tree a valuable ornamental for the garden. Yet it doesn't flower freely in all districts, and comes nearer to the perfect specimens of the Deep South of the U.S.A. in our warm southern gardens. Those plants that grow in gardens around London and in the Midlands are more often than not treated as wall shrubs; no doubt they are grown like that because the owners imagine them to be tender. *M. grandiflora* is completely hardy; but in the open garden in most of our inland gardens, it grows very slowly and only after many years makes a sturdy tree not more than 20 feet tall, and much more rounded in shape than those in the south.

Even our finest specimen-plants growing freely, cannot vie with the trees one sees on lawns in the South of France, Italy and Spain. Often these trees reach a height of 50 feet or more. They are of dense, pyramidal form and flower freely and much earlier than the English plants. Normally, our trees (whether grown as trees or as wall shrubs) bloom comparatively late – round about August. In the Deep South of America (its habitat) *M. grandiflora* is at its best in May. On the French and the Italian Riviera, where it is a great show plant, the flowers open in June.

The tallest, finest trees are the wild ones found in wooded country in the southern States of the U.S.A. where they go up to a height of 80 or 90 feet. They grow as far south as Florida, and in Alabama, Louisiana, South Carolina and Georgia and as far West as Texas. An eighteenth century botanist described the plant as 'growing only in cool and shady places, where the soil, composed of brown mould, is loose, deep and fertile. These tracts lie contiguous to the great swamps which are found on the borders of the rivers, and in the middle of the pine barrens, or form themselves a part of those swamps; but it is never seen in the long and narrow marshes called branch swamps, which traverse the barrens in every direction, and in which the miry soil is shallow, with a bed of white quartz or sand beneath.'

Soil conditions for this remarkable evergreen tree are important: a deep, loamy, leafy soil is wanted, and it must never dry out during the plant's early years; yet if it is to flower freely in the open garden, as a tree, propitiousness of climate is even more important. It needs plenty of warm sunshine.

Its seed seldom ripens in Britain; but in the warm south, mature trees bear as many as 400 cones, each containing about 40 seeds. The plant is propagated either by seed or by layering.

The seedlings have produced many fine garden varieties. Some of the finest are: Var. FERRUGINEA; this has brownish felt on the underside of the leaves, which is very conspicuous and well-developed. Var. GLORIOSA is rare in English gardens and has broad leaves, and flowers as much as 14 inches across, composed of unusually thick, fleshy petals. Var. LANCEOLATA, mostly called the *Exmouth Magnolia*, since it is said to have originated in a garden in Exmouth. The leaves, brownish-red beneath, are narrower than those of the type plant; the plant flowers at a younger age and is hardier than any of the others. Var. UNDULATA has broad leaves, waved at the margins.

The variety I would choose for this district (30 miles west of London) would be the *Exmouth Magnolia*, the hardiest of all the *grandiflora* Magnolias. Even so, it would be more successful trained on a south or a south-west wall than grown as a tree in the open garden.

These Magnolias are easy to train; the foreright branches or growths which stick out untidily are simply pruned back to the main stem in September. Not all these growths should be removed, though, or much of the character of the plant will be destroyed.

These shrubs cost about 21*s*. each.

Few gardeners recommend *Magnolia delavayi* for inland gardens; it is much more tender than *M. grandiflora* and needs a warmer climate than we get here, though planted against a wall, it will survive most winters. There is a good specimen growing near a wall at Kew Botanic Gardens.

But if it is to be seen to best advantage (say, in the middle of a lawn), then it must have a place sheltered from cold winds and frost. Cornwall, Devon and the Isle of Wight are the best districts for it.

It makes a spreading, flat-topped tree, about 30 feet tall, and has very fine leaves, the largest 14 inches long by 8 inches wide; they are a dull green above and glaucous and downy beneath. The flowers are cup-shaped, a creamy-white and fragrant. Mr. G. H. Johnstone, the author of a book on the Asiatic Magnolias, says of this species: 'It would appear to flower at about 9 to 10 years from seed . . . ' And another expert states that it is so easy to layer that stock can always be kept in hand in case of zero frosts in the near future.

Cultivated specimens seldom flower freely in this country. As regards soil, it thrives well where there is chalk, provided the soil is deep, loamy and well drained.

The species was introduced in 1899 by Wilson. Its habitat is Yunnan, China, growing at altitudes from 4500 to 7500 feet. It opens its fragrant flowers towards the evening. The plant has the same curious habit under cultivation. Most shrub specialists can supply this *Magnolia.*

*Quercus ilex* is known as the Common Evergreen Oak; most gardeners know it, or they have heard of it, even if they've never seen it. It is fairly common in the south and south-west of England but seldom if ever seen in cold northern and eastern districts, where doubtless it wouldn't prosper at all. It comes from the warm Mediterranean region and needs a sheltered place and warm, deep, loamy soil on the light side. During a severe frosty spell it loses most of its leaves; but normally it sheds those of the previous year in May or June.

I doubt very much whether anyone today would ever grow it, for it is one of the giants amongst our cultivated evergreen trees, often reaching a height of 80 or 90 feet and making an enormously wide spreading head or top. It is best reserved for estate and parkland planting. But it can be adapted to restricted spaces by pruning it into smaller shapes and it is amenable to any amount of clipping. For that reason it makes a fine evergreen hedge (up to any height) and should be pruned occasionally between June and October. I have seen this Oak in the south cut and trained as a topiary hedge – a simple undulating top which wasn't difficult to keep trim and neat. It is not as good, however, as the Yews for topiary-work.

The leaves are very variable in shape; they are usually narrowly oval, about 3 inches long and an inch wide; sometimes they are entire; sometimes toothed. (The popular name of this species is the Holm Oak: *Holm* is a later form of the old English *holen* meaning Holly; no doubt the toothed, Holly-like type of leaf was responsible for the name.)

The tree has no floral beauty: the male flowers come in pendulous clusters but are not conspicuous; the fruit is a nut – the acorn, from which new plants are raised.

The only defect this tree has is perhaps the shedding of the leaves of the previous year in June; this naturally makes the surrounding ground, or lawns and paths untidy. If it is planted in a wild part of a garden, say, at the edge of a woodland, the fallen leaves are much less noticeable. One method of obviating the nuisance is to plant beneath the branches a creeper such as the Irish Ivy (*Hedera hibernica*), whose large leaves will soon hide the Oak leaves as they fall among them.

The varieties of *Quercus ilex* are not well known to most gardeners and they do not appear in any of the shrub or tree catalogues I possess. Two of the best, I consider, are: Var. GENABI, with large leaves, 5 inches long, and of a leathery texture and toothed at the apex. Var. LATIFOLIA; another large-leaved variety; the leaves are also toothed but not so thick and rigid.

*Q. ilex* is the cheapest of the Oaks: a young plant can be bought for about half a guinea.

*Q. lamellosa* is decidedly on the tender side and could not be safely grown in this district. It comes from Northern India and grows at altitudes of up to 9000 feet as does *Rhododenron grande*, the giant Rhododendron with enormous leaves. The collector, Sir Joseph Hooker, called it the noblest of all Oaks. It reaches a height of 120 feet in Nature and has leaves sometimes 15 inches or more long and 9 inches wide. Ordinarily, they are about half this size. Gardeners in the warm maritime districts of Britain prize it for its magnificent evergreen leaves, and give it even there some protection during severe winter weather. In mid-winter the leaves, a dark lustrous green above and glaucous beneath are especially good to look at.

The Cork Oak, *Quercus suber* (cork) is a tall evergreen tree up to 60 feet high in warm, maritime districts; but unsuitable for inland gardens in the Home Counties. Its habitat is Portugal, Italy, the south of France and parts of North Africa. One of the features of the tree is its remarkably thick and corky outer bark (hence the popular name); from it is produced the cork used in many industries – the best quality being made into bottle corks. The leaves are ovalish, the largest about 2 inches long by an inch wide; they are a dark, glossy green above and greyish and downy beneath. The acorns ripen the first year and are said to have a sweetish taste.

There is a variety called OCCIDENTALIS, which comes from the Atlantic side of Europe and is hardier than the type. It is better adapted to cultivation in Britain than the other. Its leaves are less persistent; and its acorns take two seasons to mature.

The Tanbark Oak (from the bark tannin is obtained) is now described by botanists as *Lithocarpus densiflora.* It is a fine evergreen tree, up to 80 feet or more in height in its habitat – California and Oregon; and has dark green leathery leaves, glaucous beneath, the largest about 6 inches long and 2 inches wide. In our gardens it makes a moderate-sized tree and is something of a rarity.

I recommend the Holm Oak (*Q. ilex*) as the best ornamental evergreen Oak for our gardens – though it's no good in cold districts. Its wood, very hard and heavy, is said to equal that of the Common Oak; and the tree lives to a great age. The Oak family, like the Yew, is remarkable for the longevity of its trees and the durability of the wood.

The evergreen Oaks will no doubt appeal less to gardeners than *Magnolia grandiflora* or the common red-berried Holly. I imagine these last two will be chosen by the vast majority of gardeners on the look out for hardy evergreen trees. Those of us with inland gardens would not of course attempt to grow any of the tender ones such as the Mimosa or a Eucalyptus. We might have the right soil for them but we can't provide the climate and the weather. We can protect small plants and tiny shrubs effectually from frosts and bad weather but we would find covering up a tree or a big shrub much too difficult.

## CHAPTER FOUR

# *Camellias*

CAMELLIAS are evergreens we look at enviously when we see them in bloom in other people's gardens; or when we go to southern countries like Italy, and Spain and see them growing as tall as trees and full of flowers. Then we regard them as the most beautiful and desirable of all trees.

In Japan, China and Korea, where *Camellia japonica* grows in the wild, the plant often reaches a height of 40 feet and has a strong, straight trunk, smooth and pale green, resembling the trunk of a young Beech.

Charles Sprague Sanger, the eminent botanist and collector, who died in 1927, says in his *Forest Flora of Japan* that in Southern Japan *Camellia japonica* (the best known of the species) is a common forest plant from the sea-level to an altitude of 2,500 feet on the east coast, and grows as far north as latitude 36, where it is a dwarf bush only a few feet high. But when the soil and climate favour it, the Camellia becomes a tree 30 to 40 feet tall.

It is the varieties of this wild plant that we see in our gardens and some of us grow in hot-houses. They do not however respond well to artificial heat; it often causes the flowers to drop; Camellias are best grown in a sheltered spot out of doors, or in cold northern climates, in a well-ventilated cold greenhouse.

*C. japonica,* known to the Japanese as *Tsubaki,* was cultivated in their gardens in the 15th century; many charming seedling forms were raised, and many others were introduced into the country from China. Exchange of varieties went on between the two countries during the course of centuries, but none of the plants reached Europe till about 1800. The type plant seems to have been despatched to England by accident in a consignment of specimens and seeds of the tea-plant (*Camellia sinensis*) by the East India Company in China about the beginning of the 18th century. It was thought that the tea-plant might be cultivated successfully here as it was in the East. It is too tender however (and as an ornamental scarcely worth the space it requires); you might find an odd plant or two in our warm maritime gardens (there are some in the Temperate House at Kew); they have small white flowers and only their glossy green foliage is attractive. But *C. japonica* and the first varieties raised, such as the lovely double-white ALBA PLENA, and the red RUBRA PLENA attracted much attention and soon became favourite shrubs for the adornment of hot-houses and conservatories.

There is a large number of remarkable beautiful varieties now available from our shrub nurseries; some single, some semi-double (the best kinds for outdoor culture, by the way), and the very double ones, which are more backward in opening and seem to suffer more from frosts.

Actually, six forms have been identified, ranging from *Single* to *Formal Double*.

(1) *Single*. The flower has usually 5 to 7 petals, at most 9, which surround the stamens, sometimes an occasional one of these becoming slightly petaloid.

(2) *Semi-double*. The flower is made up of from 14 to 20 petals in two or more rows; sometimes there are as few as 9 petals. The centre is similar to that of the *Single*.

(3) *Anemone Form*. A flat flower; its centre is a convex mass of intermingling petaloids and stamens; the outer petals are in one or more rows.

(4) *Paeony Form*. The several rows of large outer petals form a deep rounded flower; the centre is similar to that of the preceding.

(5) *Rose Form*. Imbricated petals (overlapping like tiles on a roof). When the flower is fully open, the stamens are visible.

(6) *Formal double*. The flower is made up of many rows of imbricated petals; the stamens are seldom visible.

Seedlings and varieties of *C. japonica*, raised first in China and Japan hundreds of years ago, then in Europe and America (their number is inestimable) show an astonishingly wide range of colouring and form. Thousands have gone out of cultivation, but we are still left with at least 12,000 which have been recorded. The difficulty of choosing a few for a small garden is obvious. All we can do – those of us who cannot visit a Camellia nursery or attend any of the R.H.S. Shows – is

*9. Camellia jap. elegans*

*10. Berberis darwinii*

11. *Chamaecyparis Lawsoniana Var. Elwoodii.* An extremely slow-growing conifer for a small garden.

12. *Erica tetralix Var Mollis.* The cross-leaved leaf, a native plant.

to consult current shrub catalogues. We usually find in them the cream of the particular shrubs and trees we want to grow in our garden.

The following varieties have been recommended to me by a Camellia specialist.

ADOLPHE AUDUSSON (semi-double). It was awarded an A.M. in 1934. One of the best for outdoors, although in many inland gardens its flower-buds are often spoiled by cold and damp; nevertheless it is a strong grower, its leaves and new growths withstand hard frosts very well. It is one of the most popular of the blood-red Japonica Camellias. Its flowers fall without fading, after reaching maturity, covering the ground with petals.

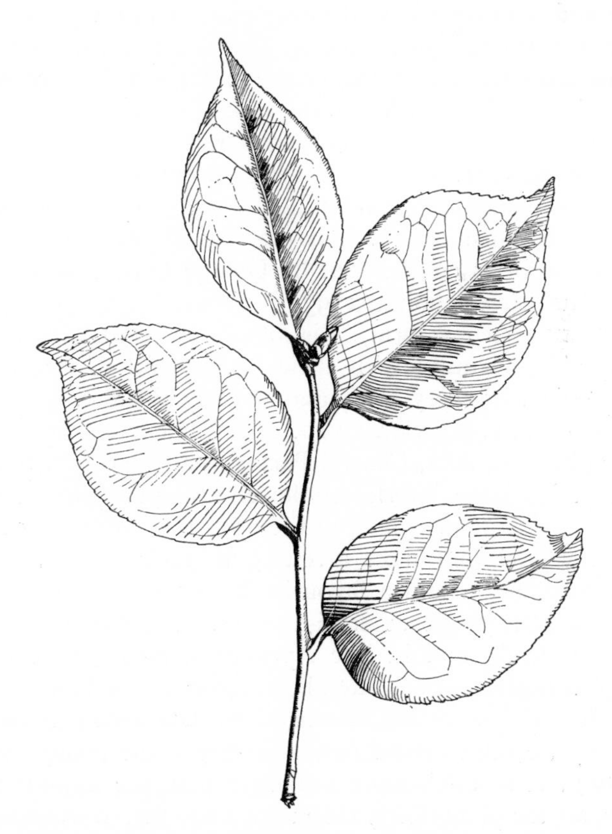

*Fig.* 6. *Camellia Japonica.* Spray of leaves with bud

ALBA PLENA (formal double). An old Chinese variety, introduced at the end of the 18th century. It has pure white waxen-like flowers, 5 inches across, which are magnificent against the burnished green leaves. (The leaves of the Japonica Camellias are ovalish in shape, a lovely glossy green and from 3 to 4 inches long; they are smooth and of a firm, leathery texture – perhaps the most beautiful of all evergreen leaves. See Fig. 6, page 65, which shows a spray of a Japonica variety from a plant growing up a north wall at Cliveden, Taplow, Bucks.) ALBA PLENA is a slow grower and difficult to propagate. Cleft-grafting is the method used by gardeners. This variety is a good choice for out-of-doors.

ALBA SIMPLEX (single). Another white variety. Large flowers with conspicuous yellow anthers. It is among the easiest to grow and does equally well under glass or in the garden.

ALTHAEAFLORA (paeony form). This has long been cultivated in our gardens and is excellent too for a cold greenhouse. Charming red flowers. A seedling raised here and mentioned by George Don in his book *General History of Dichlamydeous Plants*, published in 1831. See the following variety.

ANEMONAEFLORA (semi-double). Lovely rose-pink flowers with paeony-like centre. This variety appears in a list of *C. japonica* forms enumerated by George Don, who gives the date of its introduction as 1793.

AREJISHI (paeony form). Big blood-red flowers, which are remarkably beautiful with their background of large glossy green leaves. It is very hardy and an early bloomer.

AUGUSTO L. L. GOUVEIA PINTO. This Camellia originated in a garden in Beira Alta, Central Portugal, at the end of the 19th century. The large, imbricated flowers are a pure pink, when the plant is grown under glass; in the open they are touched with violet-lavender and most arresting in their beauty. It is a mid-season flower and a favourite florists' Camellia.

CAMPBELLII (single or semi-double). It makes a roundish, compact shrub, and in late April is covered with exquisite rose-pink flowers. It has often been recommended for a hedge. Even if the flowers are damaged by late spring frosts – a calamity we must expect now and then – the foliage will be beautiful. It is much more attractive than the Laurel. For a hedge, set the plants fairly close: not more than 2 feet apart.

CANDIDISSIMA (formal double). Another compact shrub. It

carries an abundance of pure white flowers early in the year; it was introduced as long ago as 1861 and still holds its own with any of the many new varieties.

D. HERZILIA DE FREITAS MAGALHAES (incomplete double). Another glorious Camellia from Portugal. The red flowers rather resemble those of the other variety mentioned above, and are similarly touched with violet-lavender. According to J. Moreira da Silva, who raised the plant, it often carries red and mauve flowers at the same time. It was raised in 1925 from seed collected from beneath other Camellias. Apparently some Camellias can be grafted with different varieties and carry different flowers at the same time. The following report of a gardener concerning his skill at grafting greenhouse varieties back in early Victorian times is worth giving in full. He says:

'There are several large Camellias at Woodhall that have not been shifted these 5 years, and they are still in high health, having always produced above a hundred fine large flowers every year. Six years ago I shifted a single Camellia from a 12-inch pot into a tub 17 inches wide by 17 inches deep, and grafted it with two different sorts of double red, one double striped, and one double white. It is still in the same tub, and all the four sorts in high health. I have had all the four in flower at once on it, producing a fine contrast of colours. The plant is large and handsome, being 8 feet 6 inches high, and 6 feet 9 inches wide. There is another plant here 12 feet high, having upon it all the sorts I possess. They were only grafted last summer, and a number of sorts are showing flowers. Grafts of all of them have been taken, and are growing well.'

Both of the Portuguese Camellias I have mentioned are included in Mrs. Urquhart's book *The Camellia*, a superbly illustrated folio, in which the species and varieties she has chosen are described with exemplary thoroughness.

DONCKELARII. An old catalogue of Marchant's Nursery calls it 'One of the hardiest of all Camellias for outdoor planting.' Well formed semi-double deep red flowers; free flowering. The colour has been variously described as Cherry-red, Turkey-red . . . The white variegation in the petals varies, as does the shade of red. In acid soils the red is more intense; in soils only slightly acid (or slightly alkaline) it is paler. The plant was first mentioned in *L'Horticulteur Belge* in 1834.

ELEGANS. An old favourite, with big, light red flowers measuring 5½-inches in diameter. (Sometimes listed in old catalogues as CHANDLERI ELEGANS.) It is one of the oldest and loved by every Camellia-fancier. It is the progeny of ANEMONEFLORA and VARIEGATA, which are both old Japonica variants.

EXIMEA (formal double). It is an old variety, known in England at the beginning of the 19th century. It is easy to grow and does especially well in a pot in a cold greenhouse, where its crimson flowers open about February. Equally good for outside but later in bloom.

FRAU MINNA SEIDEL (formal double). This plant is known in Japan (whence it was introduced by T. J. Seidel in 1893) as USU-OTOME, which means *Pale Maiden.* The flowers are smallish, pink, fading to white before they fall, and are much in demand by florists. It makes a superb show-piece for the conservatory or winter-garden, grown in a tub or a pot. The plant is easily raised from cuttings.

FRED SANDER (semi-double). Raised in the Belgian nurseries of F. Sander et Fils. The flowers, Turkey-red, or crimson, are medium-sized, the petals waved, are in rows, surrounding a mass of stamens. (A.M. in 1921.)

GAUNTLETTI (semi-double). It is often called by its Japanese name, SODE-GAKUSHI. This white-flowered Camellia is a good shrub for growing in a pot or a tub and it also does well out of doors.

GLOIRE DE NANTES (semi-double). This variety is recommended for planting out of doors in gardens in the London district. It has large rose-pink flowers, with conspicuous centres of deep yellow stamens.

HANA-FUKI (semi-double. Large cup-shaped flowers). It was introduced into England from Japan in 1939; some years previously into the U.S.A., where it was re-named MRS. HOWARD ASPER. The flower is singular among the Japonica varieties in being rather like those of some of the Magnolia blooms, with their recurved petals. These petals are a delightful shade of rose-pink and surround a prominent cluster of white filaments tipped with yellow.

HATSU-SAKURA (single). It has an exceptionally large flower, 6 inches across; the petals (rose-pink) are big and beautifully formed, with a central wave; the yellow anthers very prominent.

The shrub is hardy in southern gardens and blooms early. Regarded as among the finest of all the singles. It costs a little more than the other Japonica varieties – in 1966, from 25*s*. to 35*s*. a plant.

JUPITER (single). In a garden near London I have seen this Camellia planted close to a wall facing north-west, the main stems pressed against the brick-work and spreading out fan-like towards the top, where there was a superabundance of growth. It is one of the most reliable varieties for planting out of doors. It has medium to large flowers of a geranium red, with darker veining on the petals, which are broad and overlapping.

KIMBERLEY (single). A.M. in 1934. A variety probably of Japanese origin. The flowers are a brilliant red in colour and composed of 5 to 6 large, thickish petals, which surround a wide, contracting cluster of golden yellow stamens. And as an excellent foil there are the large, deep glossy green leaves. They are shallowly-serrated at the edge.

LADY CLARE (semi-double). Recommended for the garden, though regarded as too tender by some, except in warm sheltered gardens. There are several magnificent specimens at Leonardslee (Sussex). Large rose-pink flowers against large, dark green leaves. About 15 petals surrounding a centre of golden-yellow stamens. It is not in bloom as long as many of the other Japonica varieties.

LATIFOLIA (semi-double). A late bloomer and somehow its flowers always seem to catch the spring frosts. Many people like to grow it in a cold greenhouse. I knew a gardener who forced it, in a moderate temperature, and had it in bloom from October till January. The plant was grown in a tub and kept in the greenhouse all through the spring and summer months (then without heat). But the flowers did not last long after they had opened. Normally of course the outdoor flowers last longer than those of most other plants, excepting the Chrysanthemum and the Carnation. In America Camellias, when cut, are kept fresh and beautiful for many weeks in the ice-box.

MAGNOLIAEFLORA (semi-double). It has charming, rather tousled-looking flowers, the petals, about 18, channeled and recurving, surrounding an erect cluster of golden-yellow stamens. The flowers are about 4 inches in diameter and of a lovely blush pink colour. The plant makes an upright shrub of compact habit and blooms freely. In Japan, the country of its origin, it is known as HAGO-ROMO.

MATHIOTIANA (formal double). This is perfectly hardy and makes a wide-spreading shrub. Nevertheless many collectors prefer to grow it in a tub indoors so that its large, deep crimson flowers shall not be damaged by frost and damp weather – two conditions which do more damage to Camellia flowers than anything else.

MATHIOTIANA ALBA (formal double). In this form the flowers are white. Although a hardy plant, it is, like the above, often grown indoors.

MATHIOTIANA ROSEA (formal double). It has large, rose-pink flowers. Again, a hardy variety which is often grown under glass for the sake of the flowers. In many cold, northern districts of this country Camellias must be housed under glass if they are to give a show of flowers unsullied by bad weather. The greenhouse must be well ventilated and no heat should be given, except during a spell of intense cold and when the flowers happen to be opening or are just showing colour (in the bud). Prolonged artificial heat enervates the vigour of the plants and soon begins to tell; ultimately the shrubs suffer.

NAGASAKI (semi-double). A hardy variety from Japan, where the plant is called MIKEN-JAKU. The flowers are big, of a deep crimson colour, each flower composed of 9 petals slightly waved at the margins; some of the petals are blotched with white; the stamens are intermixed with a few petaloids. The deep green glossy foliage is especially beautiful.

NOBILISSIMA (paeony form). A very old Camellia which blooms early (February and March in the south); it is best housed in most districts in a cold greenhouse – I have seen it used for indoor decoration : in a pot and standing in a hall entrance. It has a self-white flower, small to medium-sized, with a high centre of mixed petaloids, twisted and folded, and conspicuous golden-yellow stamens.

RUBESCENS MAJOR (formal double). Around London it is best grown in a cold greenhouse for the sake of its glorious deep rose-red flowers. They are about 4 inches wide, the inner petals folding inward and forming a rose-bud-like centre. Propagation is effected by cleft-grafting on seedlings of *C. japonica* stocks.

TRICOLOR (semi-double). An uncommonly beautiful variegated flower. Sometimes it is white with red markings;

sometimes pink with deep carmine. The original plant, introduced by Siebold from Japan in 1830, had white flowers striped with pink and red. It has sported into several forms: TRICOLOR PINK: TRICOLOR RED: TRICOLOR FOLKI. They are characterised by their narrow leaves twisted at the centre.

YUKI-BOTAN (semi-double). A favourite variety in the U.S.A., where it was introduced from Japan in 1930; some magnificent specimens grow in California. A flower, arresting in the beauty of its structure of pure glistening white waxy petals surrounding a large centre of golden-yellow stamens.

A good collection of Japonica Camellias may be seen at Kew, growing outside, planted near a tall brick wall; they are in flower about March.

Most of the varieties I have described here will be found in current catalogues; it is a good selection, I think. Many equally as fine have been raised within the past decade in the U.S.A. and in Europe. Several are known to gardeners here in England; but not many; they have been omitted perforce from the above list.

Before describing any other garden varieties, let us look at some of the species. They are not so striking as most of the Rhododendron species; and there are comparatively few of them. And of the 82 species recognized, not more than about half a dozen are listed in catalogues. The wild plants are eclipsed in beauty by the numerous variants derived from them.

The most renowned is *Camellia sinensis* (Chinese), the Tea Plant, which was cultivated by the Chinese centuries before the Christian era. The plant is a native of Upper Assam, N. East India, where special cultivated varieties grow in the tea plantations. The type plant has narrow, dull green leaves and small fragrant white flowers. It has no ornamental value in our gardens, neither can it or its varieties be cultivated as economic plants in our climate. Some gardeners in the warm southern counties grow it as a curiosity.

Perhaps the most beautiful is *C. reticulata* (reticulated or net-veined; the name referring to the venation of the leaves, which is clearly visible, enabling one to identify the plant very easily).

The late Lord Aberconway regarded it as the finest of all the species, and according to Marchant (Nurseries) it is known as the Queen of Camellias. The flowers (semi-double) are a lovely rose-red and 6 inches wide; the leathery, net-veined glossy green leaves are 4 inches long and about 2 inches wide. It was introduced from China by Captain Rawes in 1820 – but it is actually a cultivated plant which he got from a garden or a nursery at some trading port, probably Canton or Amoy. The plant is known as CAPTAIN RAWES and is offered by most nurseries. The genuine wild species was not discovered however till 1912, when George Forrest collected it in open Pine forests in the hills around Tengyueh, Western Yunnan.

There at high altitudes it makes a tall shrub or tree up to 35 feet high, loosely branched, with dull green leaves, net-veined and smooth; the flowers, rose-red, have usually 6 petals, and numerous yellow stamens. It is a lovely plant and would succeed in our warmest, most sheltered gardens.

This species was first raised from seed sent by Forrest to Mr. J. C. Williams of Caerhays Castle, Cornwall, and flowered in 1932.

Mr. Sealy in his monograph of the genus suggests that the single-flowered plant should be designated 'forma *simplex*: *C. reticulata* forma *simplex*.' *C. reticulata* can be bought for about 32*s*. from any good shrub specialist.

Another very charming species (as beautiful, I think, as *C. reticulata*) is *C. saluenensis* (of a region around the Salween River). It was collected by Forrest on the Shweli-Salween divide, and in other regions of western Yunnan during a 1917–25 expedition. Plants were raised from seed he sent to the late Mr. J. C. Williams, and to him we owe the introduction of the species into cultivation.

The type plant is a shrub of from 6 to 12 feet high, densely covered with dark glossy green foliage; the rose-pink flowers, single, are made up of 6 or 7 petals about 1½ inches long, and have a cup-shaped centre of yellow stamens.

The flowers vary in colour in the wild state: white, rose, and crimson forms have been seen.

The finest specimens in England grow in Cornwall and other sheltered warm districts. The species can be obtained from any of our leading shrub nurseries and costs about 30*s*. a plant.

Hillier says of it: 'This beautiful species from West China has withstood our severest winters here (Winchester), with only slight injury, when given a carefully selected site. It resembles *C. reticulata*, but has smaller leaves and flowers, the latter being a lovely soft pink, and most profusely borne over a long period.'

A much older Camellia, which has been known to us since the beginning of the 19th century, is *C. sasanqua* (Sasan-Kuwa in Japan and China). I saw it in bloom in November in the Temperate House at Kew: a shrub about 12 feet tall, of open habit, with smallish glossy-green leaves and covered with small single pink flowers, which smelt delightfully of tea. Outside, in the garden, the shrub flowers later, and in this district more often than not is a failure, the flowers being completely destroyed by damp and frost.

The pink-flowered plant is probably a cultivated form, since the genuine wild plant has small white flowers. It is apparently widely spread in Japan and China. Some of the finest specimens to be seen in Europe grow in North Italy where the bushes reach a height of 20 feet or more, and measure nearly as much across.

Far more attractive are the varieties of the species, some of these are described on pages 78 – 79.

*Camellia cuspidata* (with a rigid point or cusp; referring to the leaves). The plant, although no great beauty, received an A.M. in 1912. It is quite decorative when well in flower; the flowers are white, single, small, and have a centre of yellow stamens; and the narrow, glossy green leaves (2 inches long) are sometimes purplish tinted.

It may be seen in the Temperate House at Kew: a tall, erect, slender shrub, quite pretty when in bloom, about April. (Hillier's have the shrub, about 25*s*. to 31*s*. 6*d*. – 1966.)

*C. japonica* (of Japan). The type plant is not listed in any catalogues I have consulted. But with so many of its beautiful varieties on the market (far superior in every way), probably nobody is particularly interested in it as a garden shrub. The species has a wider distribution than Japan only; it is found also in many parts of China and Korea. The plant reaches a height of 30 to 40 feet in its natural habitat – actually it is a smallish tree. The flower is rose-red, with 5 petals surrounding a centre of yellow stamens. The leaves, dark green above and paler beneath, are oval and from 3 to 4 inches long. The oil expressed from the seeds is used by Japanese women for dressing the hair, as is the oil of another species, namely *Camellia oleifera*. (See page 74.)

*C. maliflora* (malforned; referring to the gynaeceum or pistil of the flower). Not listed in Hillier's catalogue. It is not known in the wild and is probably of garden origin. Captain Rawes brought it to England in 1818; he is thought to have found it in a garden in some district in China. The flowers are small (1½ inches across), double and of an exquisite shade of blush-rose; the leaves a dark glossy green and about 2 inches long. The plant makes a bushy shrub, with pendulous twigs and branches, and usually reaches a height of 6 to 8 feet. It blooms round about Christmas-time and is valuable on that account; unfortunately like so many winter-flowering shrubs, it is very seldom a success out of doors in the British Isles: it is best housed. At Kew there is a fine specimen in the conservatory and may be seen in full bloom about January.

*C. oleifera* (oil-yielding). This species was for many years confounded with *C. sasanqua*, which was introduced into England about the same time as *C. oleifera* – about the beginning of the 19th century. *C. sasanqua*, however, has thinner, blunter leaves and smaller fruits. *C. oleifera* figures in the *Botanical Register* (t. 942 – 1825) and is described by Dr. Abel who found the plant growing in China as being 'of the magnitude of a moderate-sized Cherry-tree . . . and bearing a profusion of large white single blossoms . . . ' He collected the plant in south China in 1820. He says, 'It seems to flourish best in a red sandy soil on which few other plants will grow. The Chinese cultivate it in large plantations, and procure from its seed a pure esculent oil, by a very easy process.' The Chinese also use it in the manufacture of a soap which the women use for shampooing the hair.

The plant is rarely seen in cultivation in Britain. It needs a very warm, sheltered spot in a warm district. Marchant's catalogue says: 'Its richly scented, five-petalled, white flowers start to open in November and continue until February. Cut blooms placed in water last some time.' On the whole, Camellias are some of the best flowers for cutting, since they last many weeks.

*C. taliensis* (of regions adjacent to the Tali range, the Tali lake). This Camellia was first collected by Augustine Henry in 1897 at Yuanking; and in 1914 George Forrest saw it near Tali. Its habitat is Yunnan, Kweichow and Hunan, west China. Hillier's have the plant (31*s*. 6*d*. to 42*s*.) and the catalogue (1966) described it: 'An interesting new species related to *C. sinensis*, the *Tea Plant*. Leaves, bright green, Laurel-like; flowers axillary, cream with conspicuous yellow stamens.' It usually makes a shrub 10 feet high, or more, with ovalish, smooth, dark green leaves, 3 to 6 inches long, and small white flowers in the leaf axils (the upper angle between the leaf and the stem it springs from). Like the preceding species, it will thrive and flower well only in our warmest counties. It is more attractive when in bud, or when the flower-buds are about to open. In a cold greenhouse it blooms from September to December and is thus a valuable shrub for a late display of flowers.

Not many other species are in cultivation in this country. Hillier offers *C. drupifera*: 'akin to *C. sasanqua*, recently discovered at 3,000 feet on Lantan, near Hong Kong.' (1966 catalogue.) *C. granthamiana*, from Hong Kong, with large parchment white flowers. *C. hongkongensis*, a tender species carrying 2-inch wide crimson flowers with prominent bright yellow anthers. *C. tsai*: a graceful, Chinese species resembling *C. cuspidata*; small white flowers but numerous; foliage copper coloured when young. They are on the tender side and do best in a cool greenhouse. None is as lovely as any of the garden varieties. And of these most collectors regard the varieties of *Camellia reticulata* as the loveliest. These garden Camellias, so prized by gardeners today, had been in cultivation by the Chinese for many centuries. Only in recent years were they introduced into Europe and the U.S.A., and most of them were collected around Kunming, the capital of Yunnan by Mr. Ralph Peer, the American Camellia specialist, with the help of Professor H. T. Tsai of the Yunnan Botanical Institute.

The following are obtainable from any good shrub nursery. One of the best known: TAYINHUNG (synonym: SHOT SILK) – brilliant pink flowers, with wavy petals, has been acclaimed by enthusiasts here and in the U.S.A. It received an A.M. in 1952.

CHANG'S TEMPLE. A vigorous shrub of compact growth. The flowers often measure 8 inches across. They are pink, blotched white, paeony formed, with waved and spiralled petals.

MARY WILLIAMS (single). One of the many garden forms raised from seed collected by George Forrest (No. 27165) near Tengyueh in western Yunnan. The flowers are at least 4 inches wide and are composed of from 6 to 8 broad petals, which are a deep shade of crimson. The Camellia received an A.M. in 1942.

PAOCHUCHA (NOBLE PEARL). Semi-double, large deep red flowers with crinkled petals. A.M. 1952.

PAGODA. Sometimes a double flower; large and of a deep scarlet colour. The shrub blooms in mid-winter in warm, southern climates. A magnificent and world-famous specimen, many years old, grows in the gardens of the Capital Hsishan Temple in Kunming. The width of the trunk at the base is 2 feet; and the plant is over 30 feet tall. A tree which astonishes all who see it.

PROFESSOR TSAI has medium-sized, rose-pink semi-double flowers, with wavy petals.

SUPERBA (single). One of the many seedlings raised from seed collected by George Forrest. The open flower measures 4 inches across and has 8 to 10 wide-spreading petals of a deep red colour shaded on the outside with crimson.

TREWITHIN PINK. This is a well-known form, likewise raised from seed collected by Forrest. The soft-pink flowers are semi-double and measure 4 inches across.

The average price of the *reticulata* Camellias is 42*s*. a plant. You won't find any growing out of doors in inland gardens in the Home Counties, or as far north as London; for, even more than the *japonica* kinds, they need protection against cold, damp weather, and spring frosts. They flower in February and March as a rule, consequently the flowers need the warmth of the south and a place in a garden sheltered from winds. In Italy they flourish luxuriantly, growing into tall, wide shrubs covered with flowers. They are at their best during January and February.

Crosses between some of the species have resulted in many fine garden Camellias: *C. saluenensis X C. japonica* produced such lovely plants as the *X williamsii* hybrids. J. C. WILLIAMS was the first of this cross to be distributed. It has single flowers, about 4 inches across, composed of from 6 to 8 petals, an exquisite dog-rose pink, surrounding a cluster of golden-yellow stamens. The leaves are matt, not glossy. The hybrid was raised by Mr. Williams at Caerhays Castle, Cornwall. The plants he chose were a pale pink form of *C. saluenensis* (grown from seed collected by Forrest in Yunnan) and *C. japonica*; and the result was one of the loveliest of all evergreen shrubs. It is easily increased by cuttings. An important thing to remember when planting, is that all the *C. X williamsii* hybrids need staking: they have inherited the quick, tall-growing habit of the parent *C. saluenensis* and may be damaged if swayed about by winds. An occasional pruning, judiciously done, will keep the shrubs shapely and tidy.

DONATION. Called by Hillier one of the most outstanding Camellias raised in this country. (Parents: *C. saluenensis X C. japonica* DONCKELARII). Large semi-double, clear self-pink flowers, opening fully to a deep peach shade. The petals, rounded, are often slightly notched at the tips. This Camellia was introduced by Colonel Stephenson R. Clarke of Borde Hill, Sussex and received an A.M. on 25th March, 1941. Good flowering plants 12 feet high may be seen in some of our southern gardens near the sea. A specimen costs from 27*s.* 6*d.* to 63*s.*

FRANCIS HANGER (*C. saluenensis X C. japonica* ALBA SIMPLEX). Beautiful pure white single flowers, with conspicuous centres of yellow stamens. It is of upright growth and one of the hardiest. The plant was raised at Wisley (R.H.S. Gardens), and given an A.M. on April 14th, 1953.

MARY CHRISTIAN (single). A variety recommended by many specialists. Excepting only the darker pink of its flowers, the shrub resembles J. C. WILLIAMS in every way. (See page 76.)

NOVEMBER PINK. In warm maritime districts (in Cornish and Devon gardens, for instance) this variety will carry its lovely pink flowers intermittently from October to April. It resembles, then, the November Cherry (*Prunus subhirtella autumnalis*), which blooms, during the same period. The two would look good together; the taller Cherry, a deciduous tree whose branches are covered with small, semi-double whitish-pink flowers, should be behind the Camellia. Or perhaps the pink form *autumnalis rosea* would be even more striking.

CORNISH SNOW (*C. saluenensis X C. cuspidata*). Another beautiful hybrid raised at Caerhays, Cornwall, by Mr. J. C. Williams. It makes a charming garden shrub, with pure white flowers which come singly or in pairs. Each flower is composed of about 8 petals which surround a cluster of golden-yellow stamens. The leaves are small and a dark glossy green.

These hybrids flower freely, and over a long period; but

unfortunately can only be grown out of doors in the warmest parts of the country.

Most of the *C. sasanqua* varieties were raised in Japan, where for centuries they have been special favourites with gardeners. Many hundreds of different kinds are known there, but very few here; they hardly vie with the bigger, more showy *japonica* and *reticulata* varieties, which most of us prefer to grow. They are late autumn and winter bloomers; they do best (like all the Camellias) in a protected spot and are excellent as wall-shrubs. In Japan during the winter *C. sasanqua* may often be seen full of lovely pink flowers, while the ground beneath is covered with snow.

The vast majority of the varieties have single flowers. Those I describe below are well-known in the U.S.A. Most of them were imported from Japan; others were raised from seed by different shrub specialists in America.

ASAHI-GAI (single). An importation from Japan. It has a comparatively large flower – about 4 inches across, made up of 8 or 9 petals, slightly craped and of a rose-purple colour. The leaves are small and narrow and a pleasing shade of dark green.

CLEOPATRA (semi-double). The deep rose-coloured flower, with its conspicuous centre of bright yellow stamens, rather resembles the open flower of Cistus *purpureus* (see Pages 146–147,) though it is not so fragile-looking as that evanescent flower. The plant is a strong-growing vigorous shrub, very lovely when in full bloom. It came from Japan in 1929.

CRIMSON TIDE (single). Another Cistus-like flower. The plant was raised in Alabama, U.S.A., and has purplish-pink flowers.

DAYDREAM (single). A large-flowered variety. The flower is made up of from 7 to 9 petals, white in colour, becoming pinkish at the margins; the centre is a cluster of short yellow stamens. The plant was raised in a nursery in Mobile, Alabama.

HANA-YUKI (single). Because of its slow-growing habit, this is a most useful shrub for small gardens and for limited spaces. Its flowers are noticeably cupped, especially just before they are fully developed. Pure white in colour, with showy yellow stamens; and small dark green leaves.

HEBE (single). The flower is singular in form – the petals (seven) have their margins folded back, from the base to about half their length, which gives them the appearance of being widely separated from one another. They are oval when opened out. The colour is pink-purple. The leaves are a dark glossy green. The plant was raised from seed imported from Japan into the U.S.A.

HINODE-GUMO (single to semi-double). Among the most beautiful varieties that has come from Japan. The flowers are comparatively large, white flushed with soft rose-pink, the leaves narrow and dark green.

KO-GYOKU (double). This is a slow-growing *sasanqua* variety of moderate height; it was introduced from Japan about 20 years ago. The flowers are quite small, Phlox-pink in colour; their doubleness makes the plant more popular with gardeners than many of the other varieties.

NARUMI-GATA (single). The flowers are cupped at first. The petals craped, or crimped, are white flushed with pale rose at the edge, the stamens loosely arranged in the centre. Hillier's catalogue (1966) describes it: 'Probably the best *sasanqua* cultivated in Britain. Large, fragrant white flowers, tinted pink, commencing to flower in November.' They have the musty scent (or smell) characteristic of the *sasanqua* group. The shrub was imported from Japan and is a vigorous plant for sheltered gardens.

NISHEMKO (single). This variety was sent from Kew Botanical Gardens to America in 1948. The plant has smallish attractive flowers, pale pink shading off to almost white. You may see it in full bloom at Kew, usually at the end of November.

ROSEA (single). This is one of the oldest varieties known in England. The flowers, a delightful shade of rose, are medium-sized and flat when fully opened.

There is an enormous number of garden Camellias to choose from (perhaps only collectors will grow the species), and doubtless the most popular are the *japonica* kinds, one of the chief reasons being that they are some of the hardiest and most adaptable for cultivation in our gardens. Their flowers are more showy than those of the *sasanqua* varieties; true, they have not the prodigal loveliness of the *reticulata* Camellias, but they are hardier and do better in many of our inland gardens.

As I've already mentioned, there is a good show of the *japonica* varieties at Kew; and some very fine specimens may be seen in gardens around London.

As regards cultivation, all Camellias need a peaty, loamy

soil, moist and in good heart, and do not like chalk or lime. It is best on the light side, coarse sand being added to loams that are too stiff. Mulching is very important: apply a 4-inch layer of rotted leaves every April.

Camellias, like Rhododendrons, revel in partial shade, such as that provided by thin woodland. They must have some sun, however, since it helps to ripen the wood and set the flower-buds. It seems that once the plants have become well established in good soil, and have been well tended in their young state, they can tolerate plenty of sun. In Spain, Portugal and Italy, for example, there are many fine Camellias as tall as trees, some flanking long avenues in full sun.

In the British Isles there are many places where they are not a success at all when grown out of doors. The northern counties are too cold for them and they must be grown under glass. Even in the warm south the flowers will suffer from exposure to heavy rains and battering winds. But it is our wind-swept north-east regions that are immitigably hostile to the plants. The finest specimens, those nearest approaching the tree-like Camellias of southern Europe, are those that grow in south-west Ireland and in gardens along the south-west coast of Scotland.

The best time for planting is late September or May. Yet I have known gardeners plant all through the summer, the shrubs being transferred from pots to the garden and kept supplied with water till the autumn rains came.

As regards manuring, no manure of any kind should be applied to newly-planted specimens, since it keeps the ground cold and sticky all through the winter months, which often proves fatal to the young shrubs. Mulching with rotted leaves and some leaf-mould is by far the best way to feed the shrubs (rotting leaves, by the way, contain more nutrition than the actual leaf-mould); apply after a good rain or after you have soaked the ground well. When the flower-buds begin to show and there is certainly no suggestion of frost, a little weak liquid manure may be given; unfortunately this can hardly ever be done, as the plants come into flower during the coldest days. But feeding can be done all through the summer; use some well-decayed cow manure; break it up (it should be old enough to almost powder) and work it in carefully round the shrubs; do not dig it in deep, or you will disturb the roots.

13. *Juniperus Sabina Var. Pfitzeriana*—a dwarf conifer excellent for the formal garden.

14. *Juniperus Sabina Var. Tamariscifolia.*

15. *Ilex aquifolium*

16. *Cotoneaster cornubia*

For the foliage: many gardeners apply a little weak soot-water occasionally. It should be given after a good shower of rain, or after you have watered, as should the liquid manure.

Camellias make incomparably lovely hedges: set the plants about 18 inches apart. And for a sunny spot choose preferably some of the *sasanqua* shrubs such as DAINTY BESS of dense growth (rose-coloured flowers); and SEAFOAM (white). The *sasanqua* varieties do not mind plenty of sun on them; their foliage is less susceptible to sun-burn than the foliage of the *japonica* varieties.

The hedge is best left as a free-flowering hedge, I think; though some gardeners like to clip it over lightly in late spring with shears. All that is wanted is an occasional tidying with the secateurs.

If you cannot grow Camellias in your garden, you can grow them in pots and tubs, provided you have a suitable place for them. They cannot be accommodated on a window-sill or in places where a potted Azalea will stand. Ideally they are grown in cool greenhouses which are efficiently ventilated. In a house, I think the best place for them is a hall; and on warm days (in March or April) they may be stood outside for a time.

Camellias are supplied in pots and should be left in the pot, if they are to be grown indoors. They will thrive and flower profusely and require little attention apart from watering when the soil becomes dry. It should never be allowed to dry out; you can test it by scraping away a little of the surface: if it is damp, don't water; it should never be hard and powdery. The temperature of the room or the greenhouse will of course influence the condition of the soil.

Indoors it will be safe to give a little weak liquid manure once every 10 days when the flower-buds begin to show colour. Overhead spraying that moistens the foliage completely is very necessary for all indoor plants. Stand small Camellias in the sink to spray them; large ones put outside in the garden.

Watering should be far less frequent when the plants have finished flowering; stand them outside in a sheltered spot, and water when new growth commences.

Only after some years will the plants need repotting. Choose a larger pot (usually I use the next size: a 5-inch, then a 6-inch). Put a piece of broken flower-pot over the drainage-hole, if you like; use a suitable compost – loam, sand and sifted peat in equal parts (it must be fairly rich: richer than the garden soil). All new flower-pots must be well soaked before use, or they will absorb the moisture from the roots of the plants.

After the Camellia has finished flowering and the soil is dry, knock it out of its pot, stand the plant in a bucket of rain water for a day, and then re-pot it. Keep the new soil to within half an inch from the top so that you can water the plant more effectually.

Camellias are long-lived plants; some specimens in southern Europe and in Asia are well over a hundred years old; some of the tree-like kinds carry apparently a thousand flowers or more.

The ideal place for all Camellias is the warm south; in gardens in our warm southern counties they bloom freely; yet there is always the chance that the flowers may be damaged by high winds and sweeping rains. There is much to be said for growing them inside, or at least undercover. The plants themselves may not be as vigorous as those grown in the open, but the flowers will be unblemished and as good as any we see in the florists'.

## CHAPTER FIVE

# *Grey and Silver*

IN THE history and description of many plants, the date of their introduction into England is often given. A large number is said to have arrived here during the 16th century; and according to some writers, who are more specific than others, the Lavender arrived in 1568, and the Lavender Cotton or French Lavender (*Santolina chamaecyparissus*) in 1573. Elizabeth was Queen (1558-1603), and during her reign Lavender and other scented shrubs were favourite garden plants – in fact one associates Lavender and the silver-leaved Lavender Cotton with the formal gardens of the Elizabethan era.

Both plants came from the region of the Mediterranean and possibly were brought here by Woolf, gardener to Henry VIIIth (1491–1547) earlier than the dates given; he is credited with introducing the Apricot from Italy and other important fruits and plants from there and other parts of southern Europe.

Lavender, with its fragrant leaves, and sweet-smelling flower-spikes, must have become popular very quickly and no doubt was widely planted in those times. It is easy to propagate by cuttings and you can get dozens of plants from an old one.

It is an evergreen – we might call it a grey evergreen, and the Santolina a silver evergreen. There are many of these grey and silver evergreens; some however are essentially herbaceous or perennial in character and die down to ground level in the winter.

The species of Lavender are very hardy, excepting one or two which come from hot regions in Spain; and they all do well in light, sandy soil, even on the thin side, provided they get plenty of sun. But as with all young plants, it is wise to start them off well – give them a good, open sandy loam and, if you like, break up the sub-soil and loosen it with a fork.

There are about 20 species, shrubs, sub-shrubs and herbaceous perennials known, of which we grow in our gardens, I suppose, about half a dozen shrub kinds, none more than 3 feet tall and consequently suitable for small gardens. Most catalogues list about 3 different species only, and 5 or 6 varieties of the Common Lavender, each plant costing from 3*s*. to 4*s*.

The Common Lavender, *Lavandula spica* (spike-like) is as easy to grow in the open garden as the Holly-leaf Barberry, *Mahonia aquifolium* (Page 31); but it must have full sun and a light sandy soil. The more sun, it is said, the stronger the scent of the flowers. It has unfortunately a habit of losing part of the flowering stems or branches, which for some reasons wither and die. But the shrubs themselves are long-lived and just need clipping over every spring before the new growth commences. Cut out the dead pieces at the same time. The Mauvish-blue flowers come in August and are very welcome then, when there is a scarcity of flowers in the garden. They are well known – the Common Lavender hardly needs any description – ; they come on erect stalks about 18 inches long, and when cut and dried retain their fragrance for very many years. The leaves too are fragrant, and their grey-green colour associates well with many cut flowers. Sprays may be cut all through the winter for indoor decoration. Sachets of the dried flowers are still used for putting among clothes and linen; they may be bought, though of course it is a simple job to make one's own.

The oil of Lavender obtained from *L. spica* is less odoriferous than that from the species *L. vera*; this plant however is not now considered to be different from *L. spica* and is a form widely known as the Dutch Lavender.

But before describing these, let us look at some of the varieties of the Common Lavender.

The best known is probably the dwarfer NANA MUNSTEAD DWARF, with deeper lavender-coloured flowers – almost purple, in fact. It is about 18 inches high, but is less fragrant than the type plant and blooms earlier. A pathway flanked with low hedges of this shrub is a charming feature in a garden in high summer.

There is a deeper purple-flowered sort called NANA ATROPURPUREA, about 15 inches high, with lovely violet flowers. But again, the scent is not very strong.

Var. GRAPPENHALL is much taller and is regarded as the

tallest of all the varieties – in Devonshire bushes will be seen 4 feet high. It is a strong grower.

Var. ROSEA is much less common than the others and has flowers of a pale lilac-pink colour. And Var. TWICKEL PURPLE makes a neater, tidier bush than the type plant and carries bright purple flowers.

All may be increased by cuttings taken in late summer (unflowered pieces) and inserted in sandy soil under a bell-glass or a cloche. Best of all for these outdoor cuttings is a frame, especially if a large number is required.

*L. vera* mentioned above, is very similar to the Common Lavender (most botanists now regard them as the same plant); the leaves of the former are greener, and the flower-spike is often embranched. This is the lavender that is grown in the fields at Mitcham, Surrey, for the production of an essential oil used in perfumery and for the world-famous Lavender Water. Hillier lists the plant (3*s*.) and its variety NANA ALBA, a shrub not often seen in our gardens; it is about 12 inches high and has attractive white flowers.

*L. stoechas*, like *L. dentata* and *L. pedunculata*, is not as hardy as the Common Lavender, and does better in our warmer southern regions than in our inland gardens. The leaves and stems are covered with a fine greyish-green down, and the flowers are a deep purple, densely packed on short stalks. In the south it blooms earlier than the two species I have described; and in its habitat (Southern Europe, parts of Greece and North Africa) as early as April. It was cultivated in England in the 16th. century and mentioned by the herbalists Gerard and Turner in their Herbals; apparently they gave it the name of 'French Lavender,' which is one of the popular names of *Santolina chamaecyparissus* (Cotton Lavender).

The 3 species, and the varieties of the Common Lavender may be bought at most shrub nurseries. They will thrive in any ordinary garden soil, except heavy, cold clay, and don't mind the presence of lime or chalk. *L. stoechas* is much rarer than *L. spica* (the common sort). (The specific epithet *stoechas* is from *Stoechades*, the ancient name of the Iles d'Hyéres in the Mediterranean, where the plants grew. They were much valued for the medicinal substances obtained from them).

The other species are not listed in any of the current catalogues I have at hand.

*L. dentata* (dentate: toothed) known as the Tooth-leaved Lavender. It is interesting to read Gerard's comments on this plant and *L. stoechas* (1597): 'We have them in our gardens and keep them with great diligence from the injury of our cold climate, covered in winter or grown in pots and carried into houses.' I've never seen either species in any gardens in this district, or anywhere around London; though probably shrub enthusiasts and collectors have them.

*L. dentata* is a native of Spain and regions of the Mediterranean; and it also grows on the Rock of Gibraltar; the plant revels in hot, dry places – even starved soils. I doubt if it's hot enough in England for it; it needs a sheltered warm place all through the winter, or covering up to keep off the frosts.

One of its charms is its prominently-toothed leaves. They distinguish it from all other Lavenders. The flowers are a pale lavender-blue and do not smell as good as the common sort. The plant makes a pleasant little shrub from 2 to 3 feet high.

*L. pedunculata* (having a flower-stalk); and *L. lanata* (woolly) are similarly less at home in England than in the hot countries of their origin.

Both grow wild in Spain, often at high altitudes in mountainous regions, where the soil is thin and often arid and chalky. *L. lanata* is common on the Sierra Nevada in southern Spain (a mountain range 60 miles in length), and has been found there at altitudes of 6,000 feet. Travellers who have picked the flowers, have remarked on the strong fragrance; they are a bright violet colour and come in spikes at the end of stems 1 to 2 feet long. Other people travelling in these parts apparently regard the plant as a panacea for all ailments contracted in mountaineering – though I have never heard what these were. The plant blooms in July and August.

*L. pedunculata* blooms in May and June in its habitat Spain and Portugal. It is closely related to *L. stoechas*, and for many years was thought to be a variety of that plant. But its flower-spikes are somewhat broader and shorter and come at the end of much longer stalks (*peduncle* is the mainstalk of a cluster of flowers). The flowers are violet-purple in colour. It is a pleasant little shrub for the garden but needs winter protection in most districts.

*L. spica* (the Common Lavender) and one or two of its varieties are by far the most widely planted Lavenders in our gardens. They are useful grey or greyish-blue evergreen shrubs to grow, and if lightly clipped into shape, (remove all the flower-stems), they provide pleasing grey-green dwarf bushes or a low hedge which gives a very charming effect in winter when seen against a dark background of evergreen Box or Yew.

A favourite use of the Common Lavender, the 'Old English,' is for flanking paths on level ground, and for bordering the grass pathways of a terraced garden, especially those made on steep slopes facing due south, where they get sun most part of the day. One of the finest of these terraced gardens I know is, or used to be, at 'The Heights,' Marlow, overlooking the Thames Valley. The terraced-paths were bordered with Lavender which in high summer was always alive with bees. The flowers were gathered every August and packed into a large Chinese porcelain jar which was stood in the hall, when the house belonged to Mr. A. F. Lindemann, the late Lord Cherwell's father. Lavender is seen to its best advantage when used for bordering these terrace pathways; the massed bluish flowers in descending lines or borders are remarkably effective.

The most pronounced grey-silver foliage in evergreen shrubs belongs to *Santolina* and *Artemisia*. And the most popular and the best known is the so-called 'French Lavender' or 'Lavender Cotton,' *Santolina chamaecyparissus* (from *chamai*, lying on the ground; and *cyparissus*, a plant with a leaf like Cypress). *Lavandula stoechas* is also called 'French Lavender' but the name is seldom heard, since this particular Lavender is rarely seen in our gardens. 'French Lavender' is always *Santolina*.

The Lavender Cotton is among the whitest-foliaged shrubs we grow, especially in its young state. And young plants make neater bushes than those two or three years old. It has a propensity of straggling and making a lot of untidy growth after about a year; it soon becomes untidy and shabby-looking. The plant is best renewed every year by cuttings taken in late summer. Plant the pieces in sand in heat and they will root after a week or two. Keep them in pots till the following May.

The young plants make a remarkably attractive edging and should be clipped over before the tiny bright yellow flower-heads form. The foliage has an exceedingly pungent smell – particularly when the leaves are crushed – which many people don't care for.

Like the Lavender, it is a native of the Mediterranean

region and was first cultivated in Britain about the same time as that plant.

I prefer the dwarfer form called NANA, which is about 12 inches tall; it is most effective used as a low edging to a grass pathway; it needs prompt and regular clipping.

Santolinas need a light sandy soil on the poor side and full sun. The soil seems to influence the colour of the leaves and stems: the poorer the soil, the whiter the colouring.

The other species are not so well known; and one, *S. viridis* (green), called the Holy Flax, has vivid green foliage.

*S. benthamiana* is quite a rarity and has grey-greenish leaves and creamy-white flowers.

*S. neapolitana* (of the district of Naples). This species has larger leaves, which are more finely cut than those of the popular Lavender Cotton. It makes a rather untidy shrub about 2 feet high; it is best grown in poor soil in a hot sunny position which induces stronger, shorter growth; moreover it should be pruned back in late summer to encourage new shoots, which incidentally are green at first. The flowers are small and yellow, rather like those of the Lavender Cotton, and quite attractive in the summer.

*Artemisia* provides us with some excellent grey and silver-foliaged plants; and more often than not it is the perennial herbaceous kinds that are grown in our gardens. I think the one called *A. palmatum*, with its beautifully-divided silver-white leaves the best of them. During the winter the plant dies down to ground level and in April sends up its new stems again.

The best known of all the Artemisias is *A. abrotanum* (Southern Wood or Lad's Love) with greyish, feathery leaves and yellow flowers in August and September. The foliage has a pungent smell not unlike that of Lavender Cotton. But the plant is not evergreen.

The best of the evergreen shrub species is *A. tridentata* (with teeth – toothed – at the apex, referring to the leaves). It is a native of the western United States of America where, in certain regions, the wide drifts of it are called Sage Brush. Its silver-grey foliage is pleasing all through the year; the flower-heads, small and yellowish, come in arching panicles and bloom in autumn. According to some gardeners, the plant's chief attraction is its aroma, which is very noticeable after a rainy day. It is pleasant and refreshing. Many people grow the plant solely for its scent. This Artemisia makes a spreading shrub up to about 6 feet in height. It is mostly increased by cuttings of half-ripened wood inserted in sand in the propagating frame; they do not root so readily as the herbaceous kinds.

The grey-silver shrub called erroneously *Senecio greyi*, is now more often seen in our gardens, especially in the southern counties, than the Lavender Cotton. One of the reasons for this is no doubt that it makes a neater, more compact shrub than the Santolina. It is a native of New Zealand and its correct name is *Senecio laxifolius*; but names stick, and I've never heard anybody call it anything else but *greyi*. The true *S. greyi* is very similar but a much rarer plant.

Like most of the species, *S. laxifolius* does best in a sandy loam and in a warm, sunny climate. The finest specimens are seen in our coastal districts; and large shrubs will be found facing the sea, the thick, downy, leathery leaves standing up well to sea-spray, winds and weather.

Usually it makes a rounded, spreading shrub of moderate height, with clusters of smallish, bright yellow daisy-like flowers, which stand out conspicuously against the grey-silvery leaves – these are ovalish, greyish-green above and covered with soft silver-white felt beneath.

Although the plant is described by botanists as the most beautiful and most suitable of all the numerous Sencios for the garden, it is not liked by everybody. The lower branches are inclined to sprawl after a few years' growth; and the bright yellow daisy flowers are disliked by some. They are a glaring, hard colour, as are those of the Lavender Cotton, and not surprisingly many people cut them off before they develop. The white-silver foliage and stems don't harmonize with the shade of yellow – dark green or dull green does. (*Laxifolius*—*laxi*: loose or not compact; *folius*: leaves).

Various other species are offered by nurseries. *Senecio leucostachys* is a wall shrub with charming silver-white, finely divided leaves. It is too tender for the open garden in most districts.

The shrubby species of *Senecio* resemble *Olearia*, which are natives of Australasia. They are mostly grown for their daisy-like flowers; but *Olearia argophylla* (having silvery leaves), a species from New South Wales, Victoria and Tasmania, is grown for its beautiful silvery foliage, which is musk-scented – the flowers, white, are not very attractive. Unfortunately this lovely evergreen shrub is too tender for inland gardens and often needs winter protection in the south.

One doesn't want too many of these grey and silver evergreens in a garden, especially if they have a pronounced whiteness about them. In a small garden one or two would be enough. Lavender Cotton (*Santolina*) is often used in the herbaceous border as a buffer plant between flowers whose colours would otherwise clash. The *Senecio* is similarly used, though it is more suited to the wide, long borders of big gardens.

The grey foliage of Lavender shows up beautifully against the dark green of a Yew hedge. And white foliage against Yew gives a startling contrast – a little artificial-looking perhaps, yet effective in the lay-out of a formal garden.

Lavender Cotton and *Senecio laxifolius* are used at Cliveden for filling in the large geometrical beds (outlined with Box), which are set out on the grass parterre below the front (south) terrace of the house. (See page 142).

## CHAPTER SIX

# *The Heather Family*

HEATHERS are some of the most efficient of weed-smothering plants. You can have a border or part of a garden completely free of weeds by planting it with Heather. The dwarf, mat-forming kinds are best; the tall Tree-Heathers, with their erect stems or branches, are not much good for this purpose, though they are all intrinsically fine garden-plants.

Furthermore you can have some sort of Heather in bloom every day of the year – you need never be without colour all through the autumn and winter months.

Heathers or Heaths are usually divided into three groups, viz. *Erica*; *Calluna*; and *Daboecia*. They are evergreens and a great number of them make the useful low spreading type of plant.

Most of them need a lime-free soil; *Rhododendron* acid loam is ideal to plant them in; then when they are well established, they want no fertilizers and prosper and are longer lived in light sandy soils on the poor side, such as they get in their natural habitats.

In cultivation, in rich ground, they grow tall and lanky and shabby-looking, in much the same way as the Lavender Cotton does.

Winter-flowering Heathers, except the tall Tree kinds, must be lightly clipped over immediately after they have flowered; this keeps them dwarf and compact and causes them to burgeon near the lower part of the stems. If, however, you leave the plants unpruned for several years, you must cut back only one or two of the long woody stems at a time, for a too drastic pruning of the plant might kill it. I have found this invariably happens with the *Calluna* Heathers (the common Ling, which includes the Scottish White Heather); the old thick woody stems, often 2 feet long and naked except for the growth at the top, die when cut back to within a few inches of the base.

The *Erica* family comprises a vast number of species, most of them natives of the Cape of Good Hope and too tender for our gardens; the European kinds, however, are hardy and all evergreen.

Most nurseries list about a dozen different species of *Erica*, and many varieties, some of which were raised by growers and Nurseries in this country.

The easiest group to grow is no doubt *Erica carnea* and its varieties and forms – easy, primarily because they will thrive in any ordinary soil, even that in which lime is present; on the other hand, I have seen lean-looking specimens that have been growing in clay. I wouldn't recommend heavy clay for any of them.

In the wild they grow in peat and sand, sometimes more sand than peat; and they like open places such as moorland; they grow sometimes under trees but never flower profusely in shade – often not at all in deep shade. In gardens they need plenty of sun.

A substitute for peat is sifted leafmould with some coarse sand, say, one part leafmould to two parts of sand. Heathers of any of the groups will thrive in this medium.

It is not necessary to feed the plants ever; it may be necessary to soak them well the first summer if there is a drought. But do not give any kind of manure. Weak liquid manure has been known to kill practically any Heather you apply it to. (I am told by a grower that weak soot water is excellent for them; I have never tried this; but it would be best given after the soil has been well soaked.)

The species itself (*E. carnea*) is a native of Central Europe and was introduced into England about the middle of the 18th century. It is a low-growing shrublet about 10 inches high in its mature state; more often than not only half that. When in flower it makes a rounded mass of rosy-red blossom, which massed in wide drifts is a sheer delight. *E. carnea* received an A.M. in 1924.

I've never seen this plant growing in gardens, by the way; and I don't know anybody who has it. It begins to bloom in February as a rule and continues till April. There are, however, earlier varieties, and those with brighter, more beautiful flowers. No doubt the type plant has been eclipsed by its numerous varieties.

EILEEN PORTER blooms from October to April and has rich carmine red flowers. (A.M. in 1956.)

WINTER BEAUTY is often in full bloom at Christmas and has bright rose-pink flowers – white in the bud as with many of the Heathers.

Two white-flowered ones are SPRINGWOOD (A.M. 1930) and SNOW QUEEN. I don't care much for either; I find they spread very rapidly and are inclined to smother choicer varieties near them.

KING GEORGE (A.M. 1922 and A.G.M. 1932) is a special favourite with gardeners. It is a dwarf and keeps compact and has deep pink flowers which come early in the year.

RUBY GLOW has rich dark red flowers and bronzy foliage.

ATRORUBRA has deep pink flowers in March and April and is the last of the *carnea* varieties to bloom. (These plants cost about 4*s*. 6*d*. each.)

For an immediate effect, the plants are set as close as 9 inches apart and they quickly make broad patches of colour – the flowers seem unaffected by the worst frosts.

Gardeners who don't grow these Heathers would be delighted by the glowing colours they provide in mid-winter. They might like to try a drift of the bluish *Crocus sieberi* in front of the deep pink Heather KING GEORGE, and behind them a group of the hybrid *Rhododendron* PRAECOX. All flower simultaneously and in February. A magnificent show for winter, and something to make one look forward to February! You can think of other arrangements, using winter-flowering Crocuses, varieties of *Erica carnea* and perhaps a Rhododendron or a Witch Hazel (*Hamamelis*). (Thinking out some sort of planting scheme for one's garden is a good way of relaxing.)

As these Heathers get older, they form longer, spreading branches and cover quite a lot of ground; they are effectual weed smotherers. But where the plants have been set close together (for immediate effect, as I've just mentioned), some of them should be moved and planted elsewhere.

Nothing could be better for the rockery than the *E. carnea* varieties, planted singly, perhaps in a pocket, or at the foot of a boulder, the grey or buff stone affording an excellent background to the red, pink and crimson flowers. (The name *carnea* means 'flesh-coloured'.)

Several species of Heather are natives of Britain. These are the Dorset Heath, *Erica ciliaris*; the Scotch or Grey Heath, *E. cinerea*; the Cross-leaved Heath, *E. tetralix*; the Cornish Heather, *E. vagans*; besides several which are indigenous only to parts of Southern Ireland; and there are some good natural hybrid forms.

Outside the Erica family are *Culluna vulgaris* (originally *Erica vulgaris* – the common Ling, which blooms in autumn); and *Daboëcia cantabrica*, the Irish Heath or Saint Dabeoc's Heath.

All these Heathers need lime-free ground and revel in sandy peat.

*Erica vagans*, the Cornish Heather, is found in regions of South-West Europe and covers the heathland or moors in late summer and autumn with its purplish-pink tiny flowers (carried in racemes about 6 inches long.)

It may be seen colouring sunny slopes in Cornwall and the south and is an attractive feature of the landscape in those parts. It is more striking than the common paler pink Heather we find in districts near London.

In the wild it makes a low, spreading bush up to 2½ feet high and twice as much across, becoming in time sprawling and untidy.

In gardens it is usually clipped over in spring to keep it neat and more compact; continual cutting it back in this way, however, tends to make the racemes shorter; but this does no harm.

The variety GRANDIFLORA has racemes of rose-coloured flowers, often 15 inches long. It is frequently in bloom from June till the frosts come.

MRS. MAXWELL is regarded as the finest of all the varieties of *E. vagans* (A.M. 1925). It has deep cerise flowers covering its spreading 12-inch stems; it is beautiful from July to October. This is an excellent shrublet for massing in a sunny spot and will provide a patch of magnificent colour when there is little flowering in the garden. The plant is a natural hybrid from the Serpentine region of Cornwall.

The best white form I have seen so far is LYONESSE. It has pure white flowers with conspicuous brown anthers and is in bloom from late summer to the end of October. Not everybody cares for white Heather; they are best kept perhaps for the large Heather garden where they can be used in association with mixed reds and pinks of many other varieties. They are dull planted on their own, I think; and should not be chosen for small garden or plot.

Var. KEVERNENSIS is very similar to the type plant, but has larger, bell-shaped blossoms, which are an uncommonly beautiful shade of pure rose-pink.

The *vagans* Heathers are late summer and early autumn plants; so by chosing suitable varieties of these and the *carnea* Heathers, we can have a show of colour from July to about April. (*vagans* = wandering; of wide distribution.)

The hybrid *Erica X darleyensis* begins blooming here, in South Bucks., at the end of November and goes on till early May. It is a cross between *E. carnea* and *E. mediterranea* and has inherited some of the character of *E. carnea*: in its early stages it forms compact mound-like growths and can hardly be distinguished from that dwarf species. But ultimately it forms a bushy plant about 18 inches high; but it never becomes as tall and erect as the other parent, *E. mediterranea.*

For my part, I regard it as the most valuable of all the Heathers for the average garden. It grows well in ordinary soils (doesn't mind the presence of lime), and thrives remarkably when given an annual mulching of decayed leaves or leafmould. Its flowers are pink – not so striking a shade as that of any of the *carnea* varieties. Nonetheless the plant is really enchanting when seen in broad masses in late November. Plant the bluish-lilac autumn *Crocus pulchellus* in front of it. *Erica X darleyensis* is a plant which should be in every garden. (It originated in the heath nursery of J. Smith and Son, at Darley Dale, Derbyshire.)

Two varieties are offered by nurseries, viz.

GEORGE RENDALL, with deeper pink flowers. And SILBER SCHMELZE (a fascinating name: German, meaning Silver Crystals or glass beads). A free-flowering, white Heather.

*Erica ciliaris* is another native Heather and is especially plentiful in Dorset, covering large areas of common near Poole Harbour. It is found too in Cornwall and the West of Ireland; and it also occurs in parts of South-west Europe. It seems to flower most luxuriantly within reach of the sea air and is therefore not so popular with those of us who garden inland. I have found it difficult to establish in Buckinghamshire. It needs a moist, deep, leafy soil, which is open and sandy, and the plant should be clipped over every second year to keep it neat and compact. It is of straggling habit, the stems prostrate with erect flowering shoots springing from them, these shoots being from 6 to 12 inches high. The flowers, pitcher-shaped, are rose-red and come in July and last till late October.

Var. GLOBOSA is a delightful, natural form, with grey-green shoots and erect spikes of rose-pink flowers. It blooms till the frosts come.

There are several other attractive varieties. Perhaps the most striking of these is Var. MAWEANA (named for Mr. G. Maw, who found it in 1872 in Portugal). It has stiffer, slenderer flowering stems, and the plant is covered in autumn with large rose-crimson blossoms. The foliage is a darker green than that of the type plant. A very fine Heather and less straggling than the others of the *ciliaris* group. (*ciliaris* means 'fringed with hairs' and refers to the leaves.)

*E. cinerea* (grey or the colour of ashes; referring to the foliage). It has a wide distribution in Europe: from Norway down to Spain and North Italy and is common on many of our moors. To give the best display of flowers, it needs sandy peaty ground in full sun and is as a rule short-lived in cultivated soils, especially in the Thames Valley region. It benefits much from an annual clipping over in spring before the new growth commences; but the clipping must not be drastic or possibly the stems will die back completely.

There is an extraordinarily large number of varieties on the market; consequently it is difficult to make a selection for a small garden. (One mustn't forget that Heathers grow into large, spreading plants after some years: a first-year plant occupying a space only 4 inches square, may after years of growth require 2 square feet or more.)

I single out Var. C. D. EASON as one of the best. Its colour is brilliant – a luminous red. It reaches 12 inches in height and makes a neat shrublet for a limited space. A pleasant little plant with its dark green foliage when the flowers are over. (I grow it: it is inclined to get straggly after some years; but clipping keeps it neat; but too much will prevent its flowering at all; it won't flower freely in shade or even partial shade.)

Var. COCCINEA is an old variety which I can't get from the nurseries now. It has vivid red, or scarlet flowers and is one of the less vigorous Heathers. It has probably been superseded by Var. ATROSANGUINEA, which has darker red flowers and is more dwarf and compact in habit.

Var. ATRORUBENS has been described by a collector as 'A must.' The colour is a fiery red which shows up from a long distance. (A.M. 1915.)

There are several white forms: one, Var. ALBA MINOR is a good choice for rockeries, carrying its masses of pure white flowers on stems only a few inches high. It is best planted in a pocket on its own and allowed to spread where it will.

Var. ROSEA, with bright rose-red flowers, is an excellent Heather for massing. It received an A.G.M. in 1928.

These Heathers are summer and autumnal-blooming plants and among the most beautiful and useful of low-growing evergreens for a period when flowers in the garden are comparatively scarce.

Less often seen in our gardens are the following.

*Erica mackayi* (*mackaiana*) is regarded as a hybrid by some authorities. It is an attractive Heather, about a foot tall. The foliage is emerald-green and the flowers are rose-crimson; they are at their best in late summer. This Heather is found wild in Connemara, South-west Ireland; and in North-west Spain.

A better garden plant is the variety PLENA, which has double rose coloured flowers. They continue in bloom till September.

*E. tetralix*. The common name is the Cross-leaved Heath. The tiny leaves (dark green above; white beneath) comes in whorls, or rings round the stem, and are in the form of a cross.

This is another of our native Heathers and is found in many parts of the British Isles; it has a wider distribution than any other species. Broad masses of its rose-coloured flowers are a feature of many of our moorlands during the summer months – its blooming period is roughly from June to October.

About half a dozen varieties are offered by nurseries. Var. MOLLIS has light grey-green foliage and pure white flowers, which are lovely from June to late October.

For small gardens one of the red-flowered varieties is usually preferred. And I recommend RUBRA, with dark red flowers carried above the greyish foliage. It is a fine little shrub which gives a bright show of colour, even when planted on its own. (*Tetralix* is the Latin for 'a plant, Heath.)'

*Erica X watsonii* is a natural hybrid between *E. ciliaris* and *E. tetralix* and was found growing on moors near Truro by

Mr. H. C. Watson. It has rose-coloured flowers, pitcher-shaped and carried in racemes. They are lovely all through the late summer and often continue in bloom till November.

The dwarf Heathers I have described here are the best for limited spaces; and there are enough of them to furnish a large area, if a Heather Garden is wanted. In a small garden a Heather Patch, a few yards square, would be an excellent feature and provide a good show of colour for many months of the year. By leaving the faded flowers of the summer and autumn Heathers untouched, one gets an attractive brown and green effect all through the winter. This, by the way, is the correct treatment of these Heathers; they should not be pruned or clipped over till March or April. The winter varieties, as I've already mentioned (page 91), are pruned immediately they have flowered.

2

The Tree-Heathers are much less common in our gardens than the dwarf, spreading kinds. They are suitable only for big gardens and thrive best in the warmest parts of Britain. They flower much more freely there and especially within reach of the sea air.

*E. arborea* (tree-like) is the tallest and more genuinely 'tree-like' than the others. According to W. J. Bean (TREES AND SHRUBS HARDY IN THE BRITISH ISLES) there was a specimen growing at Ventnor in the Isle of Wight, which was 20 feet tall, with a trunk 2½ feet in girth near the ground. But in the average inland garden in this country, it is doubtful whether it grows much above 8 feet in height. This Heather very much resembles *E. lusitanica*, which is likewise tender. (See page 100).

*E. arborea* must have protection in gardens near London, and should be grown against a warm south wall. In any inland garden I would keep it covered throughout the winter months. The flowers, white and deliciously fragrant, come in great profusion in early spring.

There is a variety called ALPINA which is much hardier and prospers in practically any garden where there is good Heather soil which, ideally consists of peat and sand. This variety is quite distinct from the type plant, is less tall and has white flowers in early spring. All through the winter its light fresh green foliage is a cheerful sight; and the plant is worth growing for that alone. (It received an A.M. in 1962.)

As with all the Heathers, this variety is more striking when planted in a wide mass. Unfortunately, the Tree-Heathers are too large for massing in the small, modern garden.

Var. ALBA is found high up in the Mountains of Cuenco, south-east of Madrid; and the type plant is a native of South Europe, North Africa and the Caucasus. (Cost is about 10*s*. a plant.)

*E. australis* (southern or of the south). This species has been described both as a Tree-Heath and a Shrub-Heath. Hillier calls it, 'The showiest of the Tree-Heaths.' Marchant's description is, 'A splendid shrub during April and May.' I have never seen it above 3 feet tall in cultivation; and in the wild it is seldom much more than 4 feet. Its habitat is Spain and Portugal; the plant was introduced into England in 1769. People have tried it in pots in a cool greenhouse, where it has lived and flowered successfully for some years; but the colour (for which the species is famous) is never as bright and glowing as that of outdoor plants. It is the most beautiful shade of rose-red. No other Heather can approach it in the brilliancy of colour. The plant should be massed to get the most striking effect, though a single shrub is a picture when in full bloom – usually April to June. It should be given a place with a dark background of some sort.

A warm seaside garden is the ideal place for it. And for a picturesque effect in early summer, mass it on the edge of a thin woodland, with the double-flowered yellow Gorse (*Ulex europaeus plenus*). Both are about the same height. The Gorse, however, needs a dry, thin soil and full sun; and the Heather a sandy, peat soil free from lime. The Heather should be allowed to merge with the trees in the woodland. The effect of the rose-red fading into the woodland in spring is very striking. The yellow of the Gorse, planted in front or at the side, harmonizes well with the rose-red.

There is a pure white-flowered form called Var. MR. ROBERT, which was found by the late Lt. Robert Williams of Caerhays, Cornwall, in the mountains of southern Spain.

This of course is not so striking as the type plant. But it is hardier and grows taller – up to 9 feet in southern gardens.

Var. RIVERSLEA, which I have not yet seen, is according to

Hillier 'a 6-ft. high bush similar in habit to the type. Flowers fuchsia-purple'. These Heathers cost about 10*s*. each.

They may be increased by cuttings. Take small side shoots about an inch long in August and insert them in pots of sandy leafy soil. Give a gentle bottom heat, if possible; and leave them till the following spring.

Many of the hardy Heathers will root outside in a sheltered place. The prostrate stems of some kinds, if lying on light sandy soil, will form roots in time, if left undisturbed; the rooted portions should be cut off and planted very firmly where the new plants thus formed are to grow. Start them off in some sandy leafy loam and they will quickly grow into sturdy little shrubs.

*Erica canaliculata* is only suitable for gardens in the warmest maritime districts: in Cornwall, for example, it makes a fine evergreen bush up to 16 feet or more in height and carries white to pinkish flowers early in the year. The tiny, thread-like leaves are a dark green and make the plant an attractive shrub when the flowers have fallen. This Tree-Heather, a native of South Africa, was introduced into England in 1802, and is frequently grown in pots under glass, and sold as an ornamental indoor plant. I think it is one of the most handsome of the Tree-Heathers and deserves to be more widely grown in our warm southern gardens.

*Erica lusitanica* and *E. mediterranea* are both shrubby or Tree-Heathers, reaching about 10 feet in height in favourable districts. They have been described as on the tender side, but they thrive in many gardens in the Home Counties, if they are given a sheltered spot. Admittedly the finest specimens are to be seen in our warm seaside gardens, especially along the south-west coast – where some of our finest evergreen shrubs and trees grow. And they are more suitable for large gardens than for small ones. They need plenty of space to show off their beauty of colour and form; in narrow borders, for example, they look cramped and inevitably out of place.

*E. lusitanica* (of Portugal) cannot be recommended for all gardens, however; it must have some protection during very bad winters: a position near a wall perhaps, or have some protective material rigged up round it when a severe frost is imminent. Its leaves are ¼-inch long and its flowers white, though pink in the bud, giving an overall effect of pinkish-white; this is especially noticeable in March when the lower, opened flowers are white, and the buds above pink. They are at their best in March and April, covering the plant from top to bottom; but during a mild spell at the end of the year they begin to open early in January or even in December. It is one of the early spring-blooming Heathers and has a faint, pleasant scent. A leafy, sandy soil is ideal for it.

Its habitat is South-west Europe and it is common in Spain and Portugal. Although the species was introduced into England early in the 19th century, it has never become as popular as any of the dwarf spreading Heathers. Its tenderness no doubt deters many people from growing it.

*E. mediterranea* (the name is something of a misnomer, since the plant is not a native of the Mediterranean region – it comes from the South of France, Spain and Co. Galway in west Ireland). It makes a pleasant, dense shrubby Heather about 6 feet tall in most gardens; though it grows much bigger in warmer climates. It is an erect-growing plant; its slender branches are covered with rich rose-red flowers, bell-shaped with darker red anthers, exposed, as in many of the Heather flowers. They have the scent of honey when the sun is on them and are usually at their best in May. During a warm spell they begin to open as early as March.

The variety ALBA is smaller: from 2 to 3 feet high, and has fragrant pure white flowers which often open as early as February. This smaller, compact shrub is ideal for restricted spaces and does well in many northern gardens, though during a severe frost it needs some protection, as do the others. (Bracken placed among the branches and round the plant helps to preserve it).

Var. BRIGHTNESS is the deepest coloured form, and is seldom above 18 inches high. The bright rose-red flowers come early, often in January, and show up well against the grey-green foliage. The flowers are darker and retain their colour better when the shrub is planted in a partially-shady spot.

There are several other varieties: SUPERBA has been recommended by growers as one of the very best pink shrub-heathers (3 to 4 feet high) for the spring garden (February to April in bloom); and W. T. RACKLIFF, the finest white shrub-heather of the group.

I have found Var. ALBA a better shrub, however. As they bloom so early, a sheltered place is best for them. (They all cost about 5*s*. each.)

Many hundreds of lovely Heathers grow in the Province of the Cape of Good Hope; but there is scarcely one which is hardy enough to grow outside in Britain. And in our catalogues probably only one of them is ever listed. That is the species *Erica pageana* (named to perpetuate the memory of the botanical artist of Cape Town, Miss M. Page). It would be a triumph to get it to grow and thrive in one's garden, for it has singularly beautiful, buttercup-yellow flowers, and is probably the only yellow-flowered Heather we can grow outside. It should be tried however only in sheltered gardens in warm maritime districts.

Marchant's Nursery in Dorset, have it in their gardens, growing on the south-west side of a *Rhododendron* hedge in 1938 it was 2 feet tall. It blooms in April and May.

I have seen this Heather only in a cool greenhouse and was struck by the beauty of the deep yellow blossoms, which had a refreshing scent – probably more perceptible in an enclosed place than outside in the open. At Caerhays Castle, Cornwall, this Heather is given a sheltered spot where it gets plenty of sun. This lovely species is the most expensive of all the Heathers offered by nurseries; it costs about 15*s*. a plant.

*E. scoparia* (broom-like), the Mediterranean Besom Heather. This is a feathery-looking shrub up to 10 feet in height, of loose habit, and perfectly hardy – quite suitable for any garden around London. The leaves are a dark glossy green, small and thread-like (typical Heather leaves); the flowers, which come in May and June, are very small and not at all striking: it is principally as an evergreen foliage-shrub that the plant is grown. It will not tolerate lime and needs a peaty sandy soil. In the south of France its long stems are used for making besoms.

*E. terminalis* (ending or terminating). This is known as the Corsican Heather. It grows wild in Corsica, Sardinia, Spain and Italy, where plants up to 8 feet or more in height are found. But in cultivation it seems not to grow so tall; it is something of a rarity in our gardens – I have not seen it outside Kew Botanic Gardens. It blooms from June to September, or as late as October. The flowers, carried in terminal heads, are a lovely shade of pink. It is very hardy and succeeds in ordinary garden soils, and doesn't mind lime or chalk; yet this charming Heather is seldom seen in gardens. A plant can be had for 5*s*.

The last of the Tree-Heathers on my list is *Erica X veitchii*. This hybrid (*E. arborea X E. lusitanica*) originated in the nurseries of Messrs. Veitch in Exeter. It is a vigorous grower in that part of the country, but is rather too tender for most inland gardens farther north. The flowers, fragrant and pinkish-white, resemble in shape and colouring those of the parent plants. It is a tallish shrubby plant like *Erica arborea*; and its foliage is rather like that of *E. lustianica*. I have seen specimens 6 feet tall, but no taller, in gardens along the south coast. It needs a lime-free soil; it can be got from most shrub specialists. The plant received an A.M. in 1905.

3

The Scottish, and the Irish Heather are *Calluna vulgaris alba* and *Daboëcia cantabrica* respectively. The first was formerly described as *Erica vulgaris alba* and will be found under that name in some catalogues. The *Daboëcia* is closely related to *Erica*; but both differ slightly from the true *Erica* in the structure of their flowers.

The Calluna is the common Ling which covers vast areas of moorland in Scotland and the North of England. The Heath of the Yorkshire moors, where the grouse nest and feed on the young shoots. The plant no doubt which is mentioned so often in 'Wuthering Heights.'

Sprays of the so-called Scotch Heather used to be sold by street vendors in the West End of London years ago. One bought a spray of White Heather for luck.

I grow both the single and the double White Heather in my garden; they were planted some years ago in a mixture of sifted leafmould and sand, with only a little garden loam added. The double ALBA PLENA is better than the single (*Calluna vulgaris alba*). Both benefit from a mulching with leafmould every spring and should be lightly clipped over in March. They need full sun and refuse to flower at all in shade.

The single grows twice as tall as the double and is now 18 inches to 2 feet tall and a loose, straggling shrub. It needs pruning back (though not too drastically) in March. Before the flowers come, the plants are singularly fresh-looking with their soft mossy-green foliage.

There is a great number of varieties; and the best I have seen so far is Var. H. E. BEALE, with long spikes of double, rose-pink flowers resembling pink coral. But it is a failure in ordinary garden soils: it is best planted in a mixture of leaf-mould and coarse sand. It will never live long in dry soil; and it should be mulched yearly (every April) with a 6-inch layer of sifted leafmould or peat – or well-rotted leaves. On the other hand, good flowering specimens have been found growing in clay. It eventually makes a shrublet of open habit up to about 2 feet in height. It is perhaps the loveliest of all the autumn Heathers.

Var. ALPORTII has dark greyish foliage with crimson flowers which are at their best in late summer. The plant must have a lime-free, peaty soil.

For the rockery try Var. FOXII, a very dwarf Heather, with cushion-like tufts of deep green foliage and pink flowers. Plant it in a pocket of leafmould and sand.

Var. NANA, only a few inches high, with spreading branches covered with purple flowers, may be similarly grown.

Var. J. H. HAMILTON is another dwarf Heather and has full double pink flowers which bloom from late summer till the winter. It is especially good for massing in wide patches. This variety was found growing on Mt. Maughan, Yorkshire.

Bees haunt Heather patches and collect honey from the flowers and 'Heather Honey' is the best and the finest flavoured obtainable. Wild Heather has many uses and people living in isolated regions in Scotland look upon it as the most important of utilitarian plants. Years ago it was used as a thatch for cottages and for lining the walls, alternate layers of dried Heather and clay being used. Even a bed was made of Heather: layers of it, with the flowers placed upwards, were said to be as comfortable as a mattress.

The Irish Heather, *Daboëcia cantabrica*, is a native of Western Europe and is found wild in Connemara.

*Daboëcia* is a small genus, comprising but 2 species, viz. *D. azorica* (of the Azores); and the so-called Irish Heather, which has produced about half a dozen attractive varieties. They are all good evergreen shrubs for limited spaces, though

*D. azorica* is slightly tender and unsuitable for gardens north of London. In inland gardens, too, this species requires some shelter and would be best in a pocket in a warm rock-garden. Most gardeners who have succeeded with it (in the south) say it is at its best during the early summer, when the bronze-green foliage is covered with tiny, nodding flowers, bell-shaped and crimson. (The plant costs about 6*s*.)

*D. cantabrica* is taller, making a charming evergreen shrub up to about 2 feet high. It flowers from June till the autumn frosts come; and all through the winter months the dark green foliage is pleasant to see. The flowers are roughly egg-shaped, rose-purple in colour and about ½-inch long. The plant is completely hardy; and the varieties are likewise hardy enough for most gardens in this country. All these Heather-like shrubs must have a lime-free peaty soil; the two species may be raised from seed; the varieties from cuttings.

I recommend the following:

Var. ALBA, which has spikes of the purest white flowers, was found in Connemara at the beginning of the last century, and is an ideal plant for massing.

Var. ATROPURPUREA. This has rose-purple flowers, darker than those of the type plant. A fine edging plant where the soil is leafy and lime-free.

Var. PRAEGERAE: deep pink flowers in June. It is a delightful little plant for massing in front of some yellow-flowered shrub, which likes a lime-free or acid soil.

*Bruckenthalia spiculifolia* is another Heather-like plant, low-growing (about 6 inches high), with bell-shaped fragrant rose flowers which bloom in June. It needs a peaty acid soil and is often used in gardens as an undergrowth, not being particularly striking in flower. Some gardeners plant it in groups under Rhododendrons and Azaleas, where it soon spreads and covers the bare soil. This little evergreen plant helps to keep the weeds down and is worth growing under some of the taller Rhododendrons whose branches are erect. It is perfectly hardy and is a native of the mountains of East Europe and Asia Minor. It is easily raised from seed and increased by cuttings.

The species of *Phyllodoce* (with the exception of one) are difficult to establish in most of our gardens. These Heather-like shrubs revel in moist conditions – they do best in districts where there is a high rainfall. The easiest of them is *P. empetriformis* (the species referred to above); it is a native of western North America. A very hardy plant and, like all the *Phyllodoce*, it needs a moist, peaty, lime-free soil. The flowers are small, pitcher-shaped and a deep reddish-purple. I have tried it and our native *P. coerulea* in my garden, but neither gives as good a show as any of the *Erica* and *Calluna* I have. These are what we call the genuine Heathers – many are brilliant in colour, beautiful in flower and easy to grow.

## CHAPTER SEVEN

# *Confers*

NOT all conifers are enormous trees suitable only for planting in woodland and parkland or gardens of big estates. And not all of them are evergreen. The Larch is the best known deciduous conifer; another is the Ginkgo or Maidenhair Tree. There are several others, but they are rarely seen in this country.

For small gardens there are plenty of dwarf and slow-growing kinds – some indeed are too small for the open garden and are best grown in the rockery, where they won't be forgotten and neglected. *Chamaecyparis obtusa* CAESPITOSA is one of these: a tiny bush only a few inches high; an extremely slow grower; after many years it hardly adds an inch to its height. And there are many other conifers of this kind.

Some of the larger types are so slow growing that we can plant them in a limited space as permanent shrubs or small trees. And we would have to live to be very old to notice any great difference in the height and size of the plants. At Kew Botanic Gardens there is a specimen of *Chamaecyparis lawsoniana* NANA, which is a roundish bush, broader than it is high; it was planted in 1870, and today is not much above 4 feet tall. It would be a good choice for most of us with small gardens, who want to grow an attractive dwarf conifer. It is very hardy and one of the many varieties of *C. lawsoniana*, which species is a native of western North America (Oregon and California).

The Lawson Cypresses need good loamy soil and young plants must be watered freely till they are well established.

The Monkey Puzzle (*Araucaria araucana*) is another conifer that is often planted in a small garden. Usually specimens 12–15 inches high are obtained from nurseries and are often chosen for planting in the middle of a small lawn. But after years of healthy growth these young shrubs reach a height of 50 or 80 feet or more. This tree of course should be planted only in the biggest gardens. (See page 49.)

Yet another conifer often planted in a small garden is *Cupressus macrocarpa*, a quick-growing plant, usually adding a foot or more to its height every year. It is often used as a screening or a hedging plant – though it suffers by clipping; and it thrives much better near the sea.

There are, however, many dwarf and extremely slow-growing conifers that owners of small gardens can plant and they won't need topping or pruning during a lifetime.

The following is a good selection.

The Balsam Fir, *Abies balsamea*, has produced a curious mountain form called Var. HUDSONIA, which is rarely more than 2 feet high and makes a charming conifer for the rockery (the plant doesn't bear cones, by the way). It comes from the White Mountains of New Hampshire, and is far more successful in cultivation than the species, a tree up to 80 feet, which is short-lived in Britain. (For a description of the *Abies*, see pages 114–115.)

There is a dwarf, extremely slow-growing Lebanon Cedar called *Cedrus libani sargentii*; it is often planted as a lawn shrub and is sometimes grown in a large rockery. A good specimen costs about 30*s*.

*Chamaecyparis* are closely related to, and often included under, *Cupressus*. The former (known as 'False Cypresses') are distinguished chiefly by their flat branchlets and small cones. The *Cupressus* have rounder branches and larger cones.

*Chamaecyparis lawsoniana* LUTEA NANA is a slow-growing dwarf golden conifer, ideal for the rockery, and it makes a fine little plant to set behind one of the winter-blooming Heathers. It is more attractive, I think, than the wholly green Var. NANA, mentioned above. (page 107.)

Var. MINIMA, another miniature conifer. It is very compact, with its ascending branches curiously twisted sideways; and Var. MINIMA AUREA is a lovely golden-leafed shrub pyramidal shaped, with twisted branches. Ultimately it attains a height of about 4 feet.

Var. ELWOODI and Var. FLETCHERI are both extremely slow growing, but do eventually make tallish shrubs, and for that reason are not really suitable for the rockery. The latter, if grafted, reaches a height of 10 feet; but if raised from cuttings is dwarfer, seldom going above a height of 4 feet. (Some nurseries raise their plants only by cuttings; these are stronger and more permanent than grafted plants; grafting often has an effect on the character of the plants and they are also often less vigorous and healthy.)

The type plant (described on Page 118) was introduced in 1854 to Lawson's Nursery at Edinburgh.

The botanist Lindley in his *Treasury of Botany* (1866) describes *Chamaecyparis obtusa* as 'the Japanese Cypress, a very fine forest tree, 80 feet or more high.' It is a much slower-growing plant than *C. lawsoniana*; not many specimens in Britain are above 80 feet in height and they all need a lime-free moist soil.

Var. GRACILIS (slender) is one of the dwarf varieties: very slow growing – ultimately a small tree with graceful hanging branches.

Var. NANA is extremely slow too and has dark green, mossy foliage covering horizontally-tiered branches. It is one of the dwarfest of the *C. obtusa* species and a perfect shrublet for the rockery.

There are many other dwarf kinds of the Japanese Cypress; most of them are best accommodated, I think, in the rock-garden.

*C. pisifera* (pea-bearing, referring to the size of the cones). Another Cypress from Japan, and it has produced some charming dwarf and slow-growing varieties, all suitable for a limited space. I have seen the dwarf Var. NANA AUREA, with golden-coloured foliage, flourishing in many gardens around London, and it is the one I like best.

*C. thyoides* (Thuja-like) is the 'White Cypress' or 'White Cedar,' a slow-growing tree, native of eastern North America and usually found thriving in cold, boggy ground. Var. ERICOIDES (Heather-like) is one of the very best of the dwarf kinds; it is of compact habit, pyramidal-shaped, and its leaves turn bronze in winter. After many years it reaches a height of about 5 feet.

(These varieties can be obtained from any good shrub nurseries and cost about 15*s*. to 20*s*. a plant.)

The Junipers are natives of the temperate and sub-tropical regions of the northern hemisphere and provide us with some charming kinds for our gardens.

*Juniperus communis* (common, or growing in company) is found wild in many parts of Britain, often on limestone hills, but succeeds in neutral soils. All the dwarf specimens I have seen in gardens grew in leafy, loamy soils where Rhododendrons and Azaleas were flourishing.

The species does occasionally reach a height of 40 feet; but many plants under cultivation are not much above 10 feet high. The leaves are dark green and very attractive all through the winter months. (These are sharp and pointed or awl-shaped: the so-called juvenile leaf; and totally different from the other type of Juniper leaf, the adult, produced by other species, these being scale-like and not more than $\frac{1}{16}$-inch long.) And the berries are rounded and blackish-blue in colour. They are used to flavour gin; the oil, which gives the spirit its characteristic flavour, is distilled from the unripe berries. They are also used in cookery, usually along with other herbs. (See Fig. 7 showing juvenile and adult type of leaf.)

*Fig.* 7(*a*). Shows juvenile type of leaf
*Fig.* 7(*b*). An adult scale-like leaf of juniper

Var. COMPRESSA makes a slender, cone-shaped plant of very dense habit. It is one of the slowest growing of all conifers; a plant I saw in a garden near the lake at Zürich some years ago was 20 years old and not much above 12 inches tall. A delightful miniature conifer for the rockgarden.

*Juniperus conferata* (crowded, referring to the leaves which are crowded on the branches). This low, mat-forming species is a native of the sea-shores of Japan, and is found copiously among the wild plants on the sand dunes of Hakodate Bay of the island of Hokkaido. The bright green foliage is lovely all through the year, and especially so on plants growing within reach of the sea air. It is a fine, prostrate shrub for the lower parts of the rockery.

*J. horizontalis* is known as the Creeping Juniper, and is common on the shores of the Great Lakes and other parts of Eastern North America. In 1952 a shrub specialist in Enfield sent me a variety called GLAUCA, described on the label as 'a blue prostrate Conifer.' This is probably the same as Var. DOUGLASII – of a charming steel-blue colouring. It does best in moist loamy soil and does not grow (as the other species do) on limestone.

The dwarf varieties of *J. chinensis* do not appear to be so widely grown as those described above. *J. chinensis* Var. JAPONICA grows extremely slowly; bushes I saw recently in this district which were planted 20 years ago are 2 feet tall and about twice as wide. An excellent evergreen bush for a limited space. The foliage is mostly juvenile.

Var. JAPONICA AUREA is a lovely golden-yellow spreading Juniper, attractive as a single specimen growing against grey stone-work.

*J. sabina* (the Common Savin) is a native of the mountainous parts of Central and Southern Europe, where it is mostly found on limestone formations. As it seldom reaches more than 5 feet in height in our gardens, it is among the most useful evergreens to grow, especially in limy places. (In the wild, specimens have been found up to 15 feet tall.)

There are several good dwarf varieties.

Var. TAMARISCIFOLIA, known as the 'Spanish Savin,' a charming, prostrate form often used for covering sunny banks. It is also an excellent shrub for the rockery. (The name means Tamarisk-like.)

Var. VARIEGATA has some of its branchlets coloured creamy-white.

Var. PFITZERIANA, the 'Knap Hill Savin' is regarded as a hybrid form, and is a densely-branched, wide-spreading shrub, the branchlets drooping at the tips. It is especially attractive when grown as an isolated shrub in a small formal garden.

And the last of the dwarf Junipers I shall mention here is *J. squamata* Var. MEYERI, which is a blue-glaucous shrub of erect habit, and a very slow grower. A charming dwarf conifer. It was given an A.M. in May, 1931.

The genus *Picea* contains what is for many of us the most famous of all the conifers, namely the Christmas Tree: *Picea abies*. It is known as the 'Common Spruce' and the 'Norway Spruce;' the finest trees, producing the best timber, coming from Norway. The species is a native of Central and Northern Europe, but not of Britain. But it is widely grown as a forest tree, being of great economic value to us.

It is no ornament in the garden and in favourable districts where there is a consistently high rainfall, it reaches a height of 100 to 120 feet.

There is however a most attractive dwarf form called Var. CLANBRASSILIANA, which is a dense, rounded shrubby plant seldom reaching more than 3 feet in height after 20 years' growth. It is broader than it is high and makes a charming little conifer for planting singly in a round bed on a lawn. I have seen it grown in this way in gardens on the outskirts of Dublin. This variety actually originated in Ireland: in the private gardens of Tallymore, Co. Down. (The shrub is named in honour of Lord Clanbrasil, who discovered it growing in that district). Specimens varying in size can be bought for 13*s*. 6*d*. to 42*s*. a plant.

The 'Alberta Spruce' (*Picea albertiana*) is a native of western North America and has produced the pygmy form called Var. CONICA, which is regarded by growers as one of the finest of all the rock-garden conifers. But it does eventually reach a height of 5 or 6 feet – it would take about 20 years to grow as tall as that. It is of a very pleasing conical shape, broad at the base and tapering to a close top. The shape has been described as that of the old-fashioned candle-extinguisher. An excellent little evergreen for the middle of a small lawn. I have seen it

17. *Picea Omorika*—a fine conifer for a large garden.

18. Topiary Yews, for a more formal look.

*19. Camellia jap. alba simplex*

*20. Thuya plicata pyramidalis*

grown in an oak tub (not the best place for it), but it was watered freely and planted in a rich loam.

Spruce like cool moist growing conditions and are natives of most of the colder temperature regions of the northern hemisphere and cannot have too much rain.

Propagation is by seeds; when raised by cuttings, Spruce are not so good, nor so long-lived.

The Pines constitute the largest and the most important of the conifer groups or families. Compatively few, however, are suitable for the average garden; the smaller kinds are best, and for restricted spaces varieties such as *Pinus montana* Var. PUMILO are ideal (*Pinus mugo* is given by some botanists as the specific name). This is the form of the mountain Pine that is mostly found in our gardens. It is extremely hardy and suitable for any part of the country. Although in many gardens it seldom reaches more than 2 feet in height after many years of growth, old specimens have been known to grow as tall as 10 feet. The foliage is dark green and very pleasing all through the winter months; the cones are about 1½ inches long. This Pine thrives in the poorest soils, and is especially useful for covering sandy slopes. It transplants easily (most of them unfortunately do not) and it can be got from a nursery for about half a guinea.

*P. pumilo* is the 'Dwarf Siberian Pine' and comes from Japan, Manchuria, Siberia, and other cold regions of Eastern Asia. It seldom reaches more than 8 feet in height in our gardens and is often grown in the rockery. It is mostly of prostrate habit and has glaucous-green leaves, longish, needle-like, and aggregated into bundles of five.

These Pines like an open, loamy, well-drained soil. Young specimens should be planted, unless one can get from nurseries the larger kinds that have been specially shifted periodically to ensure safe transplanting to outside gardens.

*Thuja* (sometimes spelt *Thuya*) are classed with the same group of conifers as the flat-leaved type of Cypresses (*Chamaecyparis*).

*Thuja occidentalis* (known as the Arbor-vitae from eastern North America) has produced some fine dwarf garden forms.

Var. DUMOSA (compact, bushy) is a dwarf, rounded shrub seldom more than 2 feet high.

Var. RHEINGOLD ultimately reaches a height of 6 feet or so; a slow-grower, broadly pyramidal in form and with beautiful golden foliage in summer, which turns a deeper gold in the autumn.

*Thuja orientalis* is the Chinese Arbor-vitae, a native of North and West China. Like the preceding species, it has produced some lovely garden forms, among which are several charming dwarf kinds. The loveliest – in my opinion the loveliest of all the slow-growing conifers, is Var. DECUSSATA, whose glaucous foliage turns an astonishing plum-brown colour in late autumn; the foliage has the semblance of delicate threads of metal. There is a fine specimen at the Savill Gardens at Windsor, about 5 feet tall, and wonderful to see in late October. A good specimen can be bought for 15*s*.

Another very beautiful form is Var. ROSEDALIS. It is an extremely slow-growing shrub, attaining not much more than 3 feet after perhaps 20 years. It is a picturesque shrub all the year through: ovalish in shape, the foliage yellow in spring, sea-green in summer, and plum-purple in winter.

*Thuja* need a moist, loamy soil; they are completely hardy; but dryness at the roots and periods of drought are inimical to healthy growth.

The conifers I have mentioned in this section are suitable for small gardens and restricted spaces. There are many others – some beautiful dwarf Silver Firs (*Abies*); a particularly lovely miniature Incense Cedar (*Libocedrus*); a dwarf Douglas Fir. It would need a long chapter to describe them all adequately; the best are included with the large trees in the following section.

## 2

Although the species and varieties described in this section are trees, a number are slow-growing and take many years, perhaps a life-time, to reach maturity. The ultimate height of the tree in cultivation is given when it is known.

*Abies* are the Silver Firs, very beautiful ornamental trees for growing in moist climates, such as parts of Ireland and Scotland (particularly Perthshire), and in good deep loamy soils. They are mostly pyramidal in shape and remarkably symmetrical in form; very few are under 100 feet in height. *Abies* are sometimes confounded with the Spruce (*Picea*), to which they are allied. But *Abies* may be distinguished by their cones, which are always erect – those of the Spruce are pendent. The leaves of *Abies* are linear, like those of the Common Yew, and come away cleanly from the stem when pulled off; but those of the *Picea*, when pulled off, tear away some of the bark.

*Abies cephalonica* (of Cephalonia, one of the Ionian Isles). It is known as the Greek Fir and thrives in ordinary garden soils, even those containing chalk. It has sharp-pointed leaves and attractive cones, 4 to 6 inches long, of a velvety brown colour. A native of the mountains of Greece. The tree reaches a height of about 100 feet (suitable only for large gardens) and is among the easiest to grow in Britain.

*A. concolor*. This has been rightly called one of the most beautiful of all conifers. It makes a magnificent specimen tree for a large garden; the foliage is glaucous green; and the cones are first a rich plum colour, then turn brown.

In its native habitat, Colorado, Arizona, New Mexico, it attains a height of 100 feet; but is less than that under cultivation in Britain.

*A. forrestii* (named for George Forrest, who discovered it in China in 1910). It is one of the most striking of the *Abies* family, the leaves being a brilliant dark green above and pure white beneath, giving a delightful frosty glaucous effect, especially attractive in winter. It is known as Forrest's Fir and is a native of Yunnan and Szechwan, where it reaches a height of 60 feet or so. In gardens in Britain it is less than that.

*A. pinsapo* (this is the Spanish name for the species). It is known as the Spanish Fir, and is another very fine, tall Fir, suitable only for large gardens. It comes from the mountains of Granada in Southern Spain, where it flourishes luxuriantly on limestone. It is recommended for chalky soils in Britain and is handsome all the year, with its dark green foliage and the large purplish-brown cones.

*A. veitchii* (named for John Gould Veitch, who discovered it in Japan in 1860). Veitch's Silver Fir comes from Mount Fuji-Yama and does not prosper in chalky soils. It needs a moist loam in good heart, and is a tree that could be grown in a limited space: under cultivation (in Britain at least) it seldom goes above a height of 30 feet. It is undoubtedly among the most striking of all the Silver Firs, with its beautiful leaves, dark glossy green above and intensely white beneath; and the cones, cylindrical in shape, are blue-purple. The tree is better in the young stages of its growth, older specimens becoming rather lanky and thin-looking. It is a poor grower in chalky, limy soils.

Cedars are among the noblest of all conifers and eminently suitable for specimen planting. A good place for a Cedar is at the back of a lawn, where it can be viewed from a distance, and where its magnificent shape shows up to best advantage. It should not be planted amongst other trees.

The most famous kind is the Cedar of Lebanon (*Cedrus libani*), a native of Mount Lebanon and parts of the Taurus mountains. These trees are the 'Mighty Cedars of the Lord.' They are mentioned in the Bible: in the Book of Isaiah (35:2) they are referred to as 'the glory of Lebanon.' In ancient times invaders felled whole forests of the trees, till all that was left were isolated groves. Today about 400 trees, some more than 1,000 years old, are preserved as a national treasure – they are called by the Lebanese *Arz al-Rabb*, Cedars of the Lord. Behind them are the eternal snows of the mountains, and the trees are protected from animals by a high stone wall.

The Cedar of Lebanon needs a deep, loamy soil and does best in our warmer southern counties – the finest specimens will be seen there. I have known owners of quite small gardens plant a young tree on their lawns, hoping it could be kept dwarf. Pruning it might of course spoil the symmetry of the branches; but it is such a slow grower that no pruning would be necessary in any body's lifetime and one would never live to see the tree when it reached maturity.

Old trees are flat and spreading at the top and have enormous horizontal branches; their height is often well over 100 feet, and the diameter of their trunks may be 8 feet or more.

The Cedar of Lebanon is incomparably the most imposing of all the big trees we grow.

The Atlas Cedar, *C. atlantica*, is a quicker growing species. (It is a native of the Atlas Mountains, N. Africa.) This Cedar thrives in gardens near towns and cities, even in industrial districts, where the air is smoky and for many conifers decidedly noxious. The form Var. GLAUCA has foliage of an enchanting glaucous-blue colour and is among the most striking of all glaucous-blue trees. (Specimens can be bought in pots for about 30*s*. each.) There is a magnificent show of these Cedars at

Cliveden, Taplow, Buckinghamshire; the trees are in a row, planted on the west side of the parterre, below the terraced front of the house.

The leaves, $\frac{1}{2}$ inch to 1 inch long, are needle-like and silver-blue in colour; the cones 3 inches long, cylindrical and erect. (See Fig. 8.)

*Fig.* 8. Spray of leaves and a cone of the Blue Cedar

*Cephalotaxus* are seldom seen in our gardens. They have been described as Yew-like conifers; and they are allied to the Yews, which they resemble in the shape and arrangement of the leaves. Nurserymen tell me there is very little demand for these conifers (and not much for the Common Yew), probably because of their rather sombre appearance. Many people associate the Yew with churchyards and funerals. In the past Yew branches were carried by mourners in a funeral procession and put under the coffin in the grave. And according to John Ray, the naturalist (1627–1705), the Yew being an evergreen, was thus made typical of the immortality of man. Few people choose these evergreens for their gardens, especially those who have only a limited amount of room.

*Cephalotaxus* prosper in shady places and in limy soil, which must, however, be deep and loamy.

*C. drupacea*, known as the 'Japanese Plum Yew,' is a native of China and Japan, where specimens 30 feet high are found. In cultivation it is much smaller, not usually above 12 feet tall; it is an excellent shrub for a limited space; yet it remains a rarity. The fruits are egg-shaped, green, an inch long and ¾ inch wide.

*C. fortunei* (named for Robert Fortune, who introduced the plant in 1849). This species is a native of Northern China, and makes a small, handsome tree, with smallish leaves and of a rich glossy green colour. It is a striking evergreen tree, though not much more than a tall shrub in most localities, and is often planted in large gardens as a specimen shrub in a bed on a lawn.

*Chamaecyparis lawsoniana* (Lawson Cypress). The species is a native of western North America and abundant in Oregon and California. It often reaches a height of 200 feet in the wild; and its trunk near the base will measure 7 feet or more in diameter. It is probably the commonest and most popular of all conifers and more frequently seen in our gardens than any other. There are few so adaptable to the average garden; the tree is completely hardy and seems to thrive in any ordinary soil; the finest specimens, however, will be found growing in deep loam which retains its moisture through dry weather. And it does best in a moist climate.

No other conifer has produced such an astonishing number of different varieties and garden forms. One can only make a few suggestions: these Lawson Cypresses are all beautiful and very desirable garden trees.

I single out the choicest from those I've seen growing in different gardens in the country.

A favourite variety of many gardeners is the lovely 'Golden Cypress,' Var. HILLIERI, which has golden-yellow foliage, and a light, feathery appearance – a most cheerful-looking tree in winter. It should be planted somewhere where its elegant shape and delightful colouring can be seen from the windows of a living-room. (The plant can be got for about 17*s.* 6*d.*)

Var. FLETCHERI has already been recommended as a dwarf Cypress for the rockery or for a limited space in a small garden (see page 108). True, it would be a good choice for either of these places, being an exceptionally slow grower, but eventually it makes a tallish shrub. It is pyramidal in shape (not at all similar to the usual type of Lawson Cypress) and more resembles a Juniper. It has beautiful glaucous-blue feathery foliage and was awarded an F.C.C. in 1913.

Var. STEWARTII is another golden Cypress; the colour is richer on younger plants.

Var. ERECTA VIRIDIS is in my opinion the best of all the columnar varieties. It was raised at the Knap Hill Nurseries in 1855. Its erect shape and lovely green colour make it one of the best of all trees for specimen planting.

*C. nootkatensis* is known as the Nootka Cypress and also the Yellow Cypress of the western States of North America, where it occurs from Alaska to Oregon. It is similar to the Lawson tree but has more drooping branches. Any ordinary loamy soil suits this fine conifer, which is very hardy, vigorous and grows rapidly.

Var. LUTEA, with soft yellow-green foliage, is one of the best of the several garden forms.

The Hinoki Cypress of Japan (*C. obtusa*, see page 109) is highly valued in that country both as an ornamental and as a timber tree; and there it reaches a height of 120 feet or more, with a trunk 4 feet in diameter. But in Britain it is seldom much more than half that size and grows very slowly. Its reddish trunk and dark green foliage and the feathery appearance of the branches make it one of the most pleasing of all the conifers we grow. It needs a deep moist loam and does not thrive where there is lime.

Of the many varieties offered by nurseries, I plump for Var.

CRIPPSII, a small tree (up to 30 feet tall eventually), with young shoots of a charming golden-yellow colour. Furthermore, it has a dense, elegant habit of growth. (A good specimen costs about 30*s*.).

The Sarawa Cypress (*C. pisifera*) reaches a height of 150 feet in the wild. It is of more open habit than the Lawson Cypress and is not so widely planted in Britain as that tree or as *C. obtusa* (see page 109). More often than not one comes across some of the more attractive varieties, such as Var. AUREA, which has all its young shoots golden-yellow.

These Japanese Cypresses want a good loamy soil and plenty of moisture, especially in their young state; they are inclined to grow thin and straggly-looking on poor ground; clipping, which they stand well, helps to keep them more bushy. Occasional doses of weak liquid manure during the spring and summer are excellent for them.

*Cryptomeria japonica* is the Japanese Cedar, a native of China and Japan: a tall pyramidal tree, not at all well known here and not a great success in most districts. It needs primarily plenty of moisture in the soil and the atmosphere; and flourishes most luxuriantly in the warm moist valleys of South-west Ireland.

The garden forms are better known and on the whole more attractive plants. Var. ELEGANS is the best of these. The plant retains the juvenile form of leaf permanently and is of plumose habit. (The juvenile or young leaves are very soft and longer than the adult ones which are short and stiff in texture.) These young leaves are glaucous green in summer and turn a lovely bronzy-red in the autumn, which is a rare change of colouring among evergreens. This tinting alone makes the tree well worth growing. The trunk being very supple frequently allows the head of foliage to topple over and touch the ground. This often happens with trees 20 feet high. To prevent this, the top should be pruned back before the plant gets too tall.

The *Cupressus* (often called the True Cypresses) need loamy, leafy soils which are well drained; and young plants straight from the Nurseries should be given some shelter during the winter weather, till they have grown strong and tall. (The False or Flat-leaved Cypresses – *Chamaecyparis* – are described on pages 108–109; 118–119).

One of the finest of the *Cupressus* we can grow is the hybrid

*C. X leylandii*, raised at Leighton Hall, near Welshpool in 1888 – a valuable garden tree and singular in being the only known hybrid between Cypresses of the groups, *Cupressus* and *Chamaecyparis* (*Cupressus macrocarpa X Chamaecyparis* are the parents). It makes a tall, dense, pyramidal tree (sometimes columnar) and soon reaches a height of 40 feet – it is perhaps the fastest growing of all evergreens. When growing strongly, it stands up well to battering winds; and it succeeds on limy ground, provided there is a good depth of loamy soil. Few conifers makes such a reliable screening or hedging plant.

The plants are expensive to buy, however: 12*s*. 6*d*. each – pot-grown; but seed is obtainable from most shrub specialists.

This hybrid was named in honour of Mr. C. J. Leyland of Haggerston Castle, Northumberland.

*Cupressus macrocarpa*, often called the Monterey Cypress: Monterey is the district in California, which is its habitat. The species is another quick-growing Cypress, and once well established, often adds a foot to its height every year. This may be one of the reasons, if not the chief reason, why the plant is grown. As this Cypress grows older, it becomes more hardy and in gardens in the Thames Valley they go up to a height of 40 feet or so; near the sea (it likes the warm climate of the south best of all) it attains a height of 60 feet or more. They are not good for hedges in this district, 30 miles from London: they begin to deteriorate after being clipped and trimmed – much of the lower growth turns brown and finally dies off. But left to grow tall as individual trees (set perhaps 6 feet apart), they make a magnificent tall screen.

There are several garden forms, viz. Var. FASTIGIATA, a tree with erect-growing branches which make it columnar in shape.

Var. LUTEA is similar in shape to the other, but has young shoots and leaves of a delightful yellow colour.

Hillier's have a form called Var. GUADALUPENSIS, which they describe as 'A most beautiful tree for mild localities, lacking the characteristic fragrance of the species. Foliage glaucous sea-green.'

Junipers are lime-loving plants and thus of great value to people who garden on calcareous soils. They grow well in deep loam overlaying chalk, and thrive best in warm sunny situations. All the plants may be increased by cuttings.

One of the best kinds for gardens is the Chinese Juniper

(*Juniperus chinensis*) a native of Japan, Mongolia, and China, where specimens, slender, and pyramidal-shaped, 60 feet tall, are found. In exposed positions in cultivation it is of more shrubby habit. There are many attractive forms offered by nurseries. Of these, the one I have seen most often in gardens is Var. AUREA, known as 'Young's Golden Juniper,' a compact, slender variety; the young shoots and foliage are of a lovely golden-yellow colour – delightful to see in the summer. The plant was raised in Young's Nurseries at Milford, Surrey. It can be bought, pot-grown, for 21*s*. (See page 111 for dwarf varieties.)

*J. coxii* is known to the Chinese as the Coffin Juniper; the wood is some of the most durable to be obtained and is used by them for making coffins. And it has a remarkable fragrance, apparently when either burned or just simply handled.

The species was discovered in 1920 in Upper Burma by Messrs. E. H. M. Cox and R. Farrer. According to them, the tree, which reaches at least 100 feet in height, grows in rainy, wind-swept mountainous regions 10,000 feet above sea-level, and in places where there is little sun. In Britain it does better in the warm south-west countries, near the sea; but it is perfectly hardy, and good specimens grow in some of our inland gardens. *J. coxii* has been called the finest of all the Junipers and probably the finest conifer that grows. Its branchlets are a rich dark green and the leaves a glaucous blue-green colour. A magnificent evergreen tree.

*J. drupacea* is the Syrian Juniper from the mountains of Greece, from Asia Minor, and Syria. It was introduced about the middle of the 19th century and has proved to be hardier and more adaptable to our gardens than most of the other species. Trees will be found 30 feet or more high growing on lawns, where their elegant pyramidal or columnar shape is seen to best advantage. The leaves, dark green and sharply-pointed, are the largest among the Junipers, and the brownish fruits are about an inch wide. A choice evergreen for specimen planting in large gardens.

*J. recurva* is known as the Himalayan Juniper and was introduced from that region in 1830. It is praised by some growers for its graceful form and moderate size, which make it a good garden tree or tall shrub. Others, however, say that its dull green foliage gives the tree a lifeless look and detracts from its value as a garden plant. This Juniper is quite hardy and does well in gardens around London and in the Home Counties; the finest, tallest specimens will be found in warmer places like Cornwall and the Isle of Wight.

*J. virginiana.* This Juniper is commonly called the Red Cedar of North America. Growers in the British Isles have found it the hardiest and easiest to grow of the North American species. It does best in a deep loamy soil containing lime and is normally about 50 feet tall, but bigger specimens are known in our northern gardens. It has attractive grey-green glaucous foliage and grows into a broadly-pyramidal tree. Under cultivation it has produced some excellent varieties.

Var. BURKII (Burk's Red Cedar) of dense pyramidal habit is one of the most striking. Its grey-blue foliage turns bronze-purple in winter.

*Libocedrus* are closely allied to *Thuja* (see page 130). The most famous is the Incense Cedar, *Libocedrus decurrens*, which is one of the finest of all specimen trees. It grows slowly and makes a tall, columnar dark green tree, up to 50 feet high, or more, in many gardens, and has a formal look about it that few other trees have – almost as though it had been clipped to shape, to represent a solid, lofty pillar. It is especially adapted to the formal garden, and few trees give such an air of distinction as this – particularly when planted in a group. It needs a great deal of room of course when used for grouping or even for specimen planting; it is quite out of place in a small garden. In its young state it is almost as elegant as the tall, slender Italian Cypress, which one sees standing out against the sky in warm southern gardens of the Mediterranean. As far south as this the *Libocedrus* is more spreading in habit and perhaps less elegant. It is a hardy plant and thrives in deep moist loamy soils.

The species is a native of Oregon and California and was discovered by Colonel Fremont in 1846.

There is a singularly attractive dwarf form called Var. INTRICATA, with curiously-shaped branchlets. It is an extremely slow grower and a charming ornament for the rockery.

The few other species are less hardy and flourish in the warmest parts of Britain.

The Christmas Tree is the best known of the *Picea* family and if it thrives in your garden, in all probability the others will too. They like deep, loamy, moist soils and are a failure on thin chalky ground. They cannot have too much rain and they fail in town gardens and smoky atmospheres. The finest specimens of the Christmas Tree, *Picea abies*, are found in Norway, where it grows wild and where the rainfall is exceptionally high. It sometimes reaches a height of 150 feet. I have watched the progress of several young plants which were bought as Christmas Trees and after the festivities were planted in the garden – they were of course young trees with healthy roots when they were bought and were given good kitchen garden soil and plenty of water until they were well established. They are all flourishing.

As an ornamental tree this *Picea* is not as good as several others – not as fine a tree as the Serbian Spruce, *P. omorika*, for instance.

Spruces must be raised from seeds. Raising Christmas Trees for sale to the shops is a profitable hobby for people who have the room and the right soil in their gardens for them. The seeds germinate fairly quickly and the seedlings are planted out in rows in good deep moist soil. Or young trees about 9 inches tall may be bought from nurseries and planted where they are to grow permanently. This Spruce (*Picea abies*) is something of a failure here in South Bucks. It suffers particularly during the rainless summer months.

*Picea breweriana* (Brewer's Weeping Spruce) is a much better garden tree. (It was given an A.M. in 1958.) It is a native of Oregon and Northern California and was discovered by Mr. W. H. Brewer, an American botanist. Although one of the finest of the Spruces, hardy and a slow-grower (quite suitable for a moderate-sized garden) and a really good ornamental tree, it is something of a rarity in gardens. (It is also quite rare in Nature, occurring in small numbers high up in mountainous regions, at an altitude usually of 7,000 feet). Its distinctive character lies in the long, slender, hanging branchlets coming from the almost horizontal branches. They are whip-like, no thicker than a pencil. It is easily raised from seed. Or a pot-grown plant, ready to put out in the garden, can be had for a guinea.

The Yeddo Spruce, *P. jezoensis* has produced a remarkably fine smallish tree called Var. HONDOENSIS; it is much more suitable for the average garden than the type tree, which grows very tall. The variety has pale reddish brown shoots and attractive dark green foliage.

*P. omorika*, the Serbian Spruce, a native of Serbia and found copiously on limestone formations in the Drina Valley, Bosnia, does better in the Home Counties and in gardens around London, than most of the others. The young trees are of a slender, very elegant form; and the foliage is a cheerful glossy green colour. The plant grows rapidly and thrives in any good garden soil. (The form Var. NANA is a dwarf and makes a dense, rounded bush.)

The Oriental Spruce (*P. orientalis*) is often used instead of *Abies picea* for a Christmas Tree and often succeeds where the *Abies* is a failure. This Spruce comes from the Caucasus and Asia Minor and is of neat, dense habit; the leaves are an attractive brilliant dark green and are the shortest of all the tree Spruces.

Var. AUREA has golden-yellow shoots – a favourite conifer for gardens; good specimens, pot-grown and ready for planting out, can be bought for 45*s*. each. (Var. GRACILIS is a pygmy form, recommended for the rock-garden.)

The Blue Spruce, much admired by gardeners and beloved by growers of the Spruces, is *P. pungens* Var. GLAUCA. Its leaves are covered with a blue-white bloom; this colouring is more pronounced, however, in other forms – Var. ARGENTA is especially striking.

These 'blue' Spruces are at their best in their young state. Var. GLAUCA, mentioned above, is a choice conifer for a smallish garden and more suitable than the bigger type plant, which reaches a height of 100 feet or more. This tree (*P. pungens*) is a native of Colorado, Utah and Wyoming and is known as the Colorado Spruce.

Pines are described by Bean in his TREES AND SHRUBS thus: 'As garden or park trees, the Pines are of varying merit, but the best of them are among the noblest of evergreens. They do not need a rich soil so much as an open, well-drained one.'

*Pinus balfouriana* is the Fox-tail Pine of California and one of the smaller kinds suitable for restricted spaces; it grows very slowly. Its needle-like leaves are stiff and sharply pointed, about 1½ inches long and come in bundles of five. They persist often for fifteen years and being closely packed, give the tree a strong, vigorous appearance.

Another small Pine is *P. cembra**, a native of the Alps of Central Europe and Siberia. The popular name of it is the Arolla Pine and it is especially attractive in its young state – from about 8 feet to 15 feet tall. In its natural habitat, high up in the Alps, it grows to a height of 100 feet or more and is the common Fir-tree of these mountains (the *Tannenbaum* probably of Byron's *Childe Harold's Pilgrimage*). It is found at a higher altitude than any other tree, many old specimens having survived the storms of centuries.

The Japanese Red Pine (*P. densiflora*) is one the plants on which Japanese gardeners practise the curious art of dwarfing – trees in porcelain containers may be 100 years old and only a few inches tall. The species has an attractive reddish trunk and dark green foliage.

Much more frequently seen in gardens is the form Var. UMBRACULIFERA (umbrella-shaped), a miniature, flat-topped tree with tiny cones; it is said to take half a century to reach a height of 8 feet. It deserves to be more widely grown in small gardens; it appears to be a favourite conifer for growing in very big rock-gardens. (Plants cost according to size 21*s.* to 84*s.* each.)

*P. pinaster*, the Maritime Pine, is the species one sees growing in plantations around Bournemouth and, as its popular name implies, it is particularly suited to seaside districts, and to sandy soils. In its young state it grows rapidly, often making 2 feet a year; the leaves, which come in pairs and are stiff and dark green (4 to 8 inches long) are the longest of the Pines found wild in Europe. A mature tree, with its long naked dark trunk and a top of dark green foliage, is one of the most picturesque conifers we see along the coast. (*pinaster*, the Latin for 'a wild Pine').

*P. ponderosa*, known as the Western Yellow Pine, has a wide distribution in Western North America, where it often reaches a height of 200 feet. In cultivation in Britain, it is much smaller, but is among the most imposing of all the Pines we grow; it is very striking, with its long bunches of glaucous green leaves – some 10 inches in length. This conifer needs a deep loamy soil, rather sandy, with perfect drainage.

---

* The Italian name of the tree : actually *Pino cembro.*

*P. sylvestris*, commonly called the Scotch Pine, is a native of Britain and probably of most European countries, and found too in Siberia; it is more common in the wild than any other Pine. The Scotch Pine is a tall tree in nature (up to 110 feet high), a valuable timber tree; in gardens it is beautiful, especially during the winter months, with its graceful, red-tinged trunk and its grey-green foliage. The cones are 2½ inches long and conical. (See Fig. 9.)

*Fig.* 9. Leaves and cone of Pine (*Pinus sylvestris*)

There are many garden forms; one of the best is Var. AUREA, whose leaves turn golden in November and retain this colour till the spring, when they change to green again. A very beautiful Pine. Called by some gardeners the Golden Pine.

Var. PUMILO is a dwarf – a charming bush, densely-foliaged and rounded in shape.

The specific name of the giant Douglas Fir of North America is *Pseudotsuga taxifolia*, not *P. douglasii*, by which name it is known to many gardeners; the second is the more popular and likely to continue so among gardeners. This magnificent conifer is found in many regions of the Pacific seaboard and in its habitat reaches a height of 300 feet, with a trunk sometimes 12 feet in diameter. It is too big for most gardens and not suitable for dry climates. The finest specimens in the British Isles grow in the moist valleys of Perthshire.

The variety GLAUCA (known as the Colorada Douglas Fir) is a smaller tree, hardier and more suitable for our inland gardens. It has thicker leaves of a delightful glaucous green colour; and is the best of the many varieties for cultivation in Britain. Good specimens may be obtained from nurseries for about 5*s*.

The species was discovered by Menzies in 1793 and introduced some years later by the famous collector David Douglas.

The Yew (*Taxus*) is probably the best known of all our evergreen trees; and specimens up to 40 feet or more in height are seen in our old, historic gardens; yet it is much preferred for hedging than for planting as a specimen tree. (See page 130.)

The plant no doubt would be more often used for hedging, were it not so expensive and such a slow grower; it stands any amount of clipping and thrives in ordinary garden soils; many fine healthy plants grow on limy ground, both in cultivation and in the wild.

The common species, *Taxus baccata*, is usually raised from seed; it is collected when ripe, mixed with sand and then sown in light loamy soil.

The numerous varieties are increased by cuttings taken in August, small shoots being chosen and placed under cloches till roots are formed.

The foliage of the Common Yew is almost a black-green – one of the darkest greens in the garden and admirable for a background to precocious flowering shrubs such as *Viburnum fragrans*, with its small clusters of very fragrant pink-white blossoms, which begin to open in November; and especially for the Flame Flower or Scarlet Flame Nasturtium (*Tropaeolum speciosum*) to climb over. In shape, the leaves are linear, the

21. *Aucuba Japonica.* An old fashioned evergreen shrub seldom grown these days.

22. *Choisya Ternata*, the Mexican Orange Blossom.

23. Spray of *Elaeagnus Pungens* Var. *Aurea-Variegata*, a charming foliage shrub.

24. *Kalmia Latifolia*, a pink flowered, peat loving evergreen, rarely seen in our gardens.

largest about $1\frac{1}{4}$ inch long and $\frac{1}{2}$ inch wide; and usually a paler green (sometimes yellowish) beneath. (See Fig. 10.)

The yellow-leaved variety, which is most often grown in gardens, is Var. AUREA, whose leaves are first a golden-yellow, then turn green in autumn.

*Fig.* 10. Linear leaves of the Common Yew

Var. FRUCTO-LUTEO is the 'Yellow-berried Yew,' very attractive when in fruit.

Var. PYGMAEA is a miniature Yew, a beautiful little plant for the rockery. And the golden-leaved Var. ELEGANTISSIMA, which has been designated the perfect Yew for growing in a pot, is really one of the best for hedging, since it grows comparatively fast.

The Common Yew is a native of Europe, including the

British Isles, North Africa and West Asia. Other species occur in Canada; California; China; Japan.

*Taxus canadensis*, the Canadian species, is the hardiest of the Yews; it will grow and flourish where the climate is too cold for the Common Yew; but it is seldom much more than a low, spreading bush.

For topiary-hedges the Yews are unrivalled, the close, dense, black-green foliage (especially of the common variety) lends itself well to shaping with the shears and produces the neatest, trimmest forms. Topiary-work, however, is much less fashionable nowadays.

The Common Yew costs about 10*s.* 6*d.* a plant. The varieties are more expensive: from 17*s.* 6*d.* to a guinea. And specially-transplanted, larger specimens cost up to 3 guineas each.

*Thuja*, like *Taxus*, is a small genus, comprising about half a dozen species. (The dwarf forms are described on page 113.) The best tree form is *Thuja plicata*, commonly known as the Giant Thuja. This popular name may well deter people, even those with big gardens, from buying it. In the wild (North America) it is a giant: often 200 feet tall, with a trunk measuring 15 feet in diameter. But in gardens in Britain it reaches not more than 100 feet in height and is a slender, pyramidal tree, with branches curving upward at the ends, and dark glossy green leaves (scale-like); the cones are small and egg-shaped.

Some gardeners use this Thuja for hedging, keeping the plants clipped in April or September. (They will stand any amount of clipping). The deep green colour of the foliage is retained all through the year. The habitat of this species is British Columbia, Oregon, and Washington.

*T. orientalis*, the Chinese Arbor-vitae, is a native of North and West China and a fine tall shrub or small tree up to about 40 feet high. The better of the two forms in cultivation is a broadly-pyramidal tree furnished with branches from the ground. The cones are roundish, small, erect and purplish in colour.

This species needs a deep moist loamy soil and shelter from cold winds. These *Thuja* can be got for about 10*s.* 6*d.* each.

*Tsuga* are the Hemlock Firs or Spruces and in foliage resemble the Yew. They make elegant garden trees or tall shrubs, with usually horizontal branches and drooping branchlets.

*Tsuga sieboldii* is sometimes planted in gardens instead of the Common Yew; it is of a rather more cheerful hue than the dark-looking Yew tree. It will make a good specimen evergreen up to about 15 feet tall. It is found wild only in Japan. Like the other *Tsuga*, it needs moist growing conditions: deep, loamy soil which is moisture retentive (it should have a sheltered spot); and it prospers best in districts where the rainfall is high.

*T. diversifolia* is known as the Japanese Hemlock and, like *T. sieboldii*, confined in a wild state to Japan. In Nature it reaches a height of 80 feet or more, the reddish trunk being 6 feet or 7 feet in girth. In our gardens it is seldom much more than a tall shrub, neat in habit, with horizontal branches furnished with attractive bright yellow-green twigs during April. The cones are small and egg-shaped.

*T. heterophylla*, the Western Hemlock, is a native of western North America, from California to Alaska, and in these parts attains a height of 200 feet. Its Yew-like leaves are glossy green above and a pale greyish colour beneath. It is regarded by growers as the best of the genus to plant as an ornamental conifer for a big garden, where it must always be given adequate room to develop unrestricted. In a cramped place the lovely symmetry of the drooping branchlets is not seen to best advantage. Its tapering, conical shape is very pleasing. This magnificent conifer needs rich moist loam and cannot be grown in thin shallow soils. Small plants can be bought for 10*s*. each.

There are many conifers I haven't mentioned, for the simple reason that they are too tender or much too large for the average garden. The 'Kauri Pine' (*Agathis australis*) is suitable only for our warmest gardens in the south and south-west and has sometimes proved a failure even in Cornwall and Devonshire. Similarly the *Dacrydium*, Yew-like trees from Australasia, which really need a warmer climate than ours. And there are hundreds of course which are far too big: these are mostly grown for their timber in forestland; and some are used for special landscape effects in parkland on big estates. No ordinary pleasure garden could accommodate any of the giant Redwoods of California (*Sequoia sempervirens*) – these giants are found only in a small region called Redwood Creek Grove, Humboldt County, Calif. (The tallest, measured in 1964, was 367·8 feet high.)

Many of these conifers are listed in current Tree-and-Shrub catalogues, with sufficient information about their specific character and their likes and dislikes.

People who inherit these magnificent evergreen trees from past generations are very fortunate. Many, perhaps planted at the beginning of the century, have reached maturity and are now trees of noble proportions and great beauty.

I think it is likely that young people today are not much interested in growing conifers as ornamental trees for their gardens. Space restrictions anyhow, would prevent them: the small modern garden could accommodate only the dwarf kinds normally grown in the rockery. Occasionally, however, we find young seedling conifers planted in quite small gardens – there are plenty which do not go much above 20 feet in height and are of neat, compact habit. These will be enjoyed by those gardeners who plant them as, say, 2-feet saplings. For some grow reasonably fast and will at least reveal most of their beauty to the people who planted them.

A word of warning to intending growers of any of the deep-rooting conifers, or any tree, for that matter. They must not be planted near the house, since their roots, foraging for moisture, may well in time undermine the foundations and do a great deal of damage. Furthermore, evergreens shut out most of the sun from the rooms they face.

And the great difficulty for people who come into possession of the property later is felling the trees without damaging the house. Often the tree has to be removed by first cutting off the branches and then sawing or hacking off sections of the trunk. And it may not be possible to dig up all the roots, as many will have gone too far under the house.

# CHAPTER EIGHT

## *Some Bamboos*

THE name Bamboo suggests the jungle. And Bamboos are actually woody grasses which grow in the tropics and form dense evergreen thickets or undergrowth in the steaming junglelands of Asia. Some are an enormous size – as thick as a man's leg and 60 feet tall. Those we grow come from the northern parts of the Bamboo regions and are hardy enough for many gardens, provided the plants aren't exposed to cold north and east winds and that the place chosen for them is a sheltered one and reasonably warm throughout the winter. If they are exposed to cutting winds and severe frosts they lose their leaves and of course are less valuable to us then as ornamental plants in winter.

They are totally different in appearance from any other evergreens we grow. They form clumps, often thickets, of slender cane-like stems and cool-looking, elegant leaves – one often associates them with water and semi-tropical gardens. Indeed some of the smaller varieties are similar in appearance to our riverside rushes. And it is as waterside plants that they are best fitted; yet they do not survive for long in stagnant water or in badly drained wet soils, and are best grown in well-drained ground (the soil being loamy, lightish and peaty) sloping down to water – an artificial pool perhaps or a shallow brook.

The nomenclature of Bamboos is not yet finally settled and systematized; some botanists describe the different species under 3 genera; others have sub-divided these into additional genera.

The suitable hardy species we can grow in our gardens are usually listed as belonging to either, 1. *Arundinaria* or to 2. *Phyllostachys*.

*Arundinaria*. (The word is from the Latin *arundo*, or the better form *harundo*, meaning a Reed or a Cane). These

Bamboos have stems or canes round and straight, with numerous branches developing almost simultaneously from top to bottom.

*Arundinaria anceps* has been recommended, I imagine, chiefly for its hardiness: only in the severest winters does it lose its leaves. It is not so attractive as, say, *A. auricoma*. Its leaves are about 4 inches long and ½ inch wide, brilliant green above and glaucous beneath. The straight, erect canes may reach 15 feet in height, in deep moist leafy soils. They are purplish at first, then turn brownish-green. Its one defect (a defect usual in many Bamboos) is its habit of suckering: it sends out numerous under ground runners and these shoot up often some feet away from the main plant. (It is possible to restrict these rampant plants however by digging a trench round them – as one does round Horseradish to keep it from spreading over the garden.)

This Bamboo (*A. anceps*), although one of the easiest to grow, is suited only to large gardens. There I have seen it planted at the top of a slope near a natural pond, and providing a background to the tall golden-yellow *Primula florindae* (like a giant Cowslip) which spread down to the water's edge. The species is a native of the North-west Himalayas.

*A. auricoma* is much smaller, the canes reaching not more than about 4 feet in height, seldom that in most gardens. It is one of the tufted species, the stems making a tuft or clump and not suckering. The slender stems, a dark purplish-green, are about as thick as a knitting-needle and carry largish leaves (roughly 8 inches long by 1 inch wide), dark green, striped conspicuously golden-yellow.

The plant grows at Kew and is beautiful during the summer months; in many gardens, unfortunately it loses its leaves about the end of the year – perhaps this doesn't matter very much, when the plant is used (as I have seen it used) as an edging to a pool – pools and water-gardens are not very popular during the cold winter months, and seldom visited.

*A. auricoma* is a native of Japan and has been cultivated in Britain since the end of the 19th century. Until a shake-up in nomenclature, this Bamboo was for years known as *Bambusa fortunei* Var. AUREA. (Plants cost about 15*s*. 6*d*. each.)

*A. falcata* is one of the tufted kinds; a tall Bamboo up to 15 feet high in our warmest, most sheltered gardens. The canes are slender and glaucous when young and produce palish green narrow leaves about 6 inches long. This Bamboo is recommended as one of the most handsome of the not-so-hardy kinds, and an excellent plant for the semi-tropical garden. It is found on the Himalaya at 7,000 feet.

*A. fastuosa* is one of the hardiest, the foliage often being quite unharmed by the cold winter weather of our climate. This Bamboo is, however, suitable only for large gardens, attaining, as it does, a height of over 20 feet. The canes, erect and hollow, measure 2½ inches in diameter at the base, and have short branches which carry the dark, lustrous green leaves. The plant suckers, but is not so rampant as some species.

It is a native of Japan and known there as 'Narihira-dake.' According to Lord Redesdale, who was one of the leading authorities on Bamboos and the author of *The Bamboo Garden*, 'Narihira' appears as the glorious hero in a Japanese romance written in the 11th century.

The plant is one of the tallest and finest of the Bamboos we grow in Britain.

(The name *fastuosa* means proud, tall.)

*A. fortunei.* An extremely attractive short Bamboo (3 feet), with variegated leaves, dark green striped with white, although sometimes the green appears more prominent in the colouring. The canes or stems are no more than ⅛-inch in diameter; and the largest leaves are about 7 inches long.

It is regarded by most gardeners as the best of the small variegated Bamboos; the green and white markings giving a bright patch of colour through the winter in warm districts. The species comes from Japan. Although of tufted habit, it spreads rather quickly.

Propagation of Bamboos is by division of the plants in May or September. Exceptionally hard, matted clumps will have to be hacked into smallish pieces with a mattock or a pickaxe. The new plants should be brought on in pots in a warm greenhouse or a frame and kept moist.

*A. japonica.* Another Japanese species; introduced by the botanist Von Siebold in 1850 and the only hardy Bamboo grown in our gardens for many years. It has larger leaves than any other hardy species we grow (7 to 12 inches long; 1 inch to 2 inches wide), and it doesn't spread so rapidly as many do. It is a charming evergreen, with its tall slender canes (12 feet or more high), and its dark glossy green leaves, which are glaucous beneath.

This species flowered in Europe 22 years after its introduction – between 1872 and 1874. This fact is mentioned here, since the flowering of Bamboos is a phenomenon of interest to everybody who grows them. Many species die after they flower. (*A. anceps* is one of these – apparently in its native habitat it flowers and ripens its seeds). Other species are badly crippled but eventually recover; some of the Bamboos of the *Phyllostachys* Group, described on pages 137–9, behave in this way. Yet others have a certain number of canes which flower and then later perish, the non-flowering ones remaining active and healthy. (*A. auricoma* is an example.) After some years it often happens, however, that all the canes flower simultaneously, then the whole plant dies.

According to growers and collectors, it is possible to save the life of a Bamboo by immediately cutting back to ground level those canes that show signs of flowering.

Another interesting fact is that the plants belonging to one species wherever they are growing – in the tropics or in hot-houses – all flower (and then perish) simultaneously.

A special favourite with growers is *A. murielae*. It is among the hardiest, and reaches a height of 13 feet in some gardens. It forms a dense thicket of slender canes, which are leafless the first year, then the following season they carry an abundance of rich green foliage and arch gracefully outwards. A valuable evergreen plant for our gardens. It is one I recommended for most districts; and it costs about 17*s*. 6*d*. a plant. The species was named in honour of Muriel, the daughter of E. H. Wilson who discovered the plant in Western Hupeh, China, in 1907, and introduced it that year.

*A. nitida* is another Chinese species; it has very slender canes, about the thickness of a pencil. This species, one of the very best for our gardens, needs partial shade, since it soon suffers when exposed to full sun, the leaves starting to curl up and lose their fresh cool look. The canes, crowded, are a black-purple colour and reach a height of 6 to 10 feet. The biggest leaves are 3 inches long and about ½-inch wide, a glossy green above and paler and glaucous beneath. It is a charming Bamboo, delicate-looking, but perfectly hardy and flourishes in gardens in the London districts. Like the preceding species, the canes are erect and leafless the first year but become leafy and arching the following season. It is one of my favourite Bamboos for growing in the water-garden. The species was introduced into Britain via St. Petersburg (Leningrad) in 1889. (*nitida* = having a smooth, polished surface; probably referring to the leaves.)

(Large specimens can be bought for 27*s*. 6*d*. a plant.)

*A. palmata*. This is the species which some Bamboo specialists say should be in every garden. It is a handsome evergreen plant, but I prefer other Bamboos to it. It is undoubtedly one of the most common species we grow in this country. Although of moderate height (the canes about 6 feet tall), it cannot be recommended for a small garden, for it is a rampant spreader, its underground stems shooting up sometimes as much as a yard away from the main clump. But its large leaves, 13 inches long and 3 inches wide, make it one of the most handsome of the exotic-looking foliage plants for the waterside or for semi-tropical effects. The leaves are bright green above and glaucous beneath, but after a few years begin to lose their fresh green colour; the old stems should then be cut back to the ground in May; young shoots spring up again very qucikly and produce new juicy green growths and foliage. The species was introduced from Japan, its habitat, in 1889. (Some botanists now describe the plant under *Sasa senanensis nebulosa*. The Japanese botanist Nakai called it *Sasa palmata*; it has also been named *Arundinaria kumasasa*; and *A. metallica*; *Sasa* by the way, is the Japanese word for dwarf Bamboos.)

2.

*Phyllostachys*, the other group of Bamboos, differ from *Arundinaria* in having stems or canes more or less zigzag in shape and flattened on one side above the joints or internodes; and as regards the branches: only 2 or 3 develop at each joint and those at the base appear first. (In the *Arundinaria* Bamboos, the branches are numerous and are produced simultaneously from top to bottom.) The name *Phyllostachys* is from the Greek *Phyllon*, a leaf; and *Stachys*, a spike, referring to the leafy character of the flowering shoots.

*Phyllostachys castillonis*. This lovely Bamboo is a native of

Japan, where it is called *Kimmei-Chiku*, and it was introduced toward the end of the last century. The canes, about 8 feet high (or more in the warmer southern counties) are beautifully marked bright yellow and dark green; the green appearing on the flattened portion of the stems. The leaves vary in size: some are 2 to 5 inches long and ½-inch wide; others are almost twice as big. They are variegated – green striped with creamy-yellow lines – ; the foliage gives a charming effect in the semi-tropical garden. (The species flowered in 1903 and 1904; many plants died and this Bamboo is now rather rare.)

*P. henonis* has been described by Bamboo specialists as the finest and loveliest of all the *Phyllostachys*. Landscape gardeners acclaim it. And for their purposes it is invaluable. It is a perfect plant for the water-garden and also for the semi-tropical garden, where, by the way, I have seen it used as a background to some of the exotic-looking Yuccas.

In deep leafy moist soils and warm, sheltered places it is wonderfully luxuriant with its plumose masses of dark, shining green foliage. In our warm coastal districts the canes reach a height of 14 feet and the heavy foliage causes them to arch outwards.

Its habitat is Japan, from which country it was introduced in 1890. Specimens cultivated in Britain began flowering in 1900 and 5 years later every one was either dead or severely crippled; some, however, did recover, and from these, new stocks were built up.

*P. nigra*. This species is known as the Black-stemmed Bamboo (*nigra* = black or dark-coloured.) It flowered in Britain (and many other countries) between 1931 and 1935, and died almost everywhere; but some plants survived in a few places, and these provided the new stocks for propagation. *P. nigra*, a native of Japan, was the first of the *Phyllostachys* to be grown in this country. It is a magnificent evergreen for places like Cornwall and the Isle of Wight, where it may grow up to a height of 20 feet. (In inland gardens farther north the canes are seldom much more than half that size.) The leaves, 2 to 4 inches long, and about ½-inch wide, come in plumose masses, their dark green colour looking very beautiful against the slender black stems.

*P. viridi-glaucescens* (green-glaucous, referring to the foliage: bright green above; glaucous beneath). Among the finest of all hardy Bamboos; but is suitable only for large gardens. It is a vigorous species attaining a height of 16 feet, or sometimes 20 feet in our warmest districts. The canes are about ¾-inch in diameter, of a yellow-green colour (purplish at the joints), the outer ones arching gracefully outward and touching the ground. If the plant is grown near the bank of a stream, the tips carrying masses of foliage will reach the water, adding to the scenic interest of a large water-garden. It is prized by landscape gardeners who use it for semi-tropical effects.

This species, a native of China and introduced into Europe in 1846, has not yet flowered under cultivation. It is more inclined to run than any of the other species of this group: on the whole *Phyllostachys* do not spread so rapidly as the *Arundinaria*.

Are there any dwarf Bamboos suitable for a small modern garden? Most of them unfortunately are too tall or of a too spreading habit, and best suited to large spaces where they can grow unrestricted. (*P. viridi-glaucescens* will in time form a large spreading mass of stems and foliage measuring 25 feet across – about the size of a small front garden).

*P. ruscifolia* is about the best choice. It is 12 inches tall, with small glossy dark green leaves, and excellent for a damp spot, particularly in the rock-garden. It is one of the tufted Bamboos and doesn't spread rapidly. It costs about 17*s*. 6*d*. a plant.

Bamboos need a good mulching in April, especially those growing in light soils; and during the early summer they benefit from weak doses of manure water. It is best given after a shower of rain, when the ground is moist.

The plants also benefit from pruning periodically. Some gardeners cut them back to ground level every year to get rid of all the dead stems and faded brown foliage which are such an eyesore in a garden; then they hose the place where the plants are growing to thoroughly clean the ground. This is an excellent thing to do when large borders or beds of Bamboos have been planted. A bucketful of water will suffice for just one or two clumps.

Bamboos are an important feature of water- and semi-tropical-gardens. They are, by their form and elegant foliage, ideally suited to these places, and are especially attractive and refreshing to see growing by water during the hot summer months.

Less often we come across the Bamboo border, a feature liked by Bamboo collectors and probably the best way of displaying a large number of different species and varieties. The tufted kinds would be better for such a border than those that spread; these would soon overrun all the smaller, neater kinds; they would need continual inspection and constant pruning back.

A border furnished entirely with Bamboos has a rather monotonous appearance and it would be wise to introduce a few foliage plants of a different shape and form – the low-growing, broad-leaved *Hosta* (*Funkia*); the enormous-leaved ornamental Rhubarbs (*Rheum*), and flowering plants such as Primulas. And for the semi-tropical-garden, Yuccas, Cannas and some of the Agaves, tender plants which could be planted in the garden in their pots from June to September and lifted before the cold weather came.

Bamboos cannot be grown in this country as economic plants, but in their native countries there are large plantations of them, apart from those that are cut for use from the jungle-lands. These Bamboos have an astonishing number of uses. In China, in the past, it seems they were used for practically everything! By splitting the canes of some species, 30 feet long, into very thin lengths and twisting them together, efficient ropes were made. The sails of Chinese junks were made of Bamboo. Bamboos were used for nearly every article of furniture: chairs, tables, mats, screens, bedsteads, and even for the bedding – the plants had far more uses than the Heathers I have mentioned on page 104. Nowadays in Europe and America we have certain kinds of Bamboo shoots as a luxury food.

# CHAPTER NINE

## *Miscellaneous Shrubs and some Climbers*

In this final chapter will be found, first: evergreens that are well known to most gardeners – a few of them, for some reason or other, are not grown much nowadays; and second: those that are decidedly rare. (The evergreen climbers come last, since as I've already said, there are so few which are genuinely hardy and therefore suitable for the average garden.)

*Aucuba japonica*, sometimes called the Spotted Laurel, or the Variegated Laurel, was at one time perhaps the most common of all our evergreen shrubs. I know at least a dozen gardens in this district where it is growing and flourishing and the shrubs must have been planted many years ago. Nobody grows it now. And in the past it was always treated as a sort of filling-up plant: grown in front of an ugly coal-shed or some unsightly object. Even in the old days nobody took much notice of it.

It is as easy to grow as the Holly-leaf Mahonia (see page 31). It succeeds in shade, under trees (and in the drip of trees), where the ground is rooty and the soil thin; but the soil should not be quite impoverished; new, young plants must be started off in some good garden loam – once established, they will soon go ahead, and will tolerate dryness at the roots. (If this *Aucuba* bore flowers of any note – they are quite inconspicuous – I'd put the shrub in garden value before the Mahonia.)

Height of the shrub: 6 to 10 feet. Large leaves glossy green; spotted yellow in the female form; deep green in the male. The first Aucuba grown in this country (in 1783) was the variety called MACULATA (blotched) – a female, variegated or spotted form which did not flower till the introduction of a male plant some 60 years later. Now both types of the shrub and many attractive forms are available. Usually in large gardens one male-flowered shrub was planted among every six females; this ensured a good show of red berries.

Some of the best forms are Var. VARIEGATA (MACULATA), the common variegated female form.

Var. CRASSIFOLIA; one of the finest male plants, with thick, broad, deep green leaves.

Var. LONGIFOLIA, with bright green long, narrow leaves – excellent for semi-tropical effects, a good plant to grow with some of the Bamboos; male and female forms are obtainable; the latter carry excellent crops of berries.

Var. PICTURATA; beautifully variegated, the leaves splashed with gold.

The varieties are easily raised by cuttings. Terminal shoots inserted in sandy soil will soon root, especially if given a gentle bottom heat.

The type plant may be raised by seed sown in autumn. But first the berries must be cleared of the outer pulp.

*Aucuba japonica* is a native of Japan and during Victorian times seems to have been very widely grown; and as a pot-plant it rivalled the *Aspidistra*, and did as well indoors as out in the open.

Box (*Buxus*) is one of the easiest of all evergreens to grow and next to the Yew perhaps the neatest and tidiest-looking of the small-leaved kinds.

It has no floral beauty (the flowers are small and dingy); and it is primarily as a foliage shrub that we value it. It is excellent for topiary-work and topiary-hedges. At Cliveden Box is used as an edging to geometrically-shaped bed on the parterre (see pages 89-90), which years ago were filled with masses of deep mauve Cat Mint (*Nepeta*).

The Common Box or Tree Box is *Buxus sempervirens* (meaning always or ever green) and will grow in any ordinary soil and flourishes on chalk and on hilly ground. It succeeds in sun or shade and is as accommodating as the Holly-leaf Mahonia (*M. aquifolium*). In time, if left unpruned, it will reach a height of 30 feet and make a good, though not a particularly striking evergreen tree; some of the garden varieties with larger leaves, or of weeping habit are better.

Normally it is kept to a bush about 6 feet high, and that is how we see it in most gardens. The tiny Box edgings are not so popular nowadays; probably the constant clipping required to keep the edging neat and tidy takes up too much time. However, the variety chosen for this ornamental edging is mostly the dwarf Var. SUFFRUTICOSA (meaning low and shrubby at the base). It seems to benefit by being clipped continually; it can be kept down permanently to 9 inches or less. Propagation is by cuttings or by division.

Var. PENDULA is a charming weeping tree and

Var. AUREA PENDULA is the Golden Weeping Box.

One of the best large-leaved forms is Var. LATIFOLIA MACULATA.

*Buxus sempervirens* is a native of Europe, North Africa and West Asia; but it is doubtful whether it occurs in Britain.

*Buxus wallichiana* is a native of the north-western Himalaya, where it attains tree-like size. In our gardens it seldom reaches more than 8 feet in height, and is best suited to places like Cornwall, Devonshire and the Isle of Wight. It has larger leaves than the other kinds of Box, some measuring 2½ inches in length.

This species is a very slow grower and provides a superior dense, hard wood almost as close and heavy as ebony. It is, or was, in great demand by the wood carver.

*Ceanothus* are well known for their blue flowers and the hybrid GLOIRE DE VERSAILLES is probably the best known. The evergreen species and varieties are not so often seen perhaps; but their flowers are equally lovely and as true a blue as those of the deciduous hybrids. Pure blue or true blue is rare in shrubs and trees. The *Rhododendron* species *R. augustinii* (Page 23) is one of the bluest of the hardy evergreens we grow, though the colour is not a pure blue: not as genuinely blue as most of the *Ceanothus* flowers.

*Ceanothus* are natives of North America, particularly of the coastal regions of California, where they often attain to the size of large trees. In cultivation they are much smaller and in many of our gardens usually shrub-like.

*Ceanothus thyrsiflorus* is the hardiest and one of the choicest of the species. It is called the Californian Lilac. The name is commonly used for the *Ceanothus*, the reason being no doubt that the flowers come in panicles, Lilac-shaped in many of the plants, but smaller and usually scentless.

This species is tree-like in its habitat, the Santa Cruz Mountains of California, where it reaches a height of 40 feet tree up to about 30 feet high and in the north is a charming blue-flowered shrub for growing up a wall.

The flowers are a delightful shade of pale blue and come in clusters or panicles 1 to 3 inches long; these are surmounted by the growing leafy shoots of the current season. The leaves are small and a deep glossy green.

When in full bloom *C. thyrsiflorus* is one of the loveliest of the few blue-flowered evergreen shrubs available for our gardens. It is at its best in May. This species may be taken as representative of the early blooming *Ceanothus* (some bloom in late summer and autumn).

The early blooming kinds are pruned immediately they have finished flowering; they flower on the growths made the preceding year.

Shrubs planted in the open garden just need their longest growths topping to keep the plants tidy. On walls, harder pruning is necessary to keep them in shape: the side shoots of the past summer's growth are cut back to 3 or 4 buds of the base (*thyrsiflorus* = a thyrse, which is a kind of dense panicle like that of the Lilac).

*C. X burkwoodii* is a hybrid from *C. floribundus X C.* Var. INDIGO). This is a late flowerer, blooming from July to October and it and other late-blooming kinds are pruned in March. They flower on shoots made during the current year. In pruning these *Ceanothus*, the thin weak shoots are cut out; and the strong shoots made the preceding summer are cut back to about half their length.

The flowers of *C. X burkwoodii* are a rich bright blue and come in small panicles about 2½ inches long. The leaves are oval in shape, a shining green above and greyish and downy beneath – the largest about 1½ inches long. This charming evergreen makes a fine leafy bush about 5 feet high.

The plant was raised at the Burkwood and Skipworth Nursery, Kingston-on-Thames. It likes full sun, and is perfectly hardy. I have seen it in gardens near London, growing both in the open and against a wall. C. X AUTUMN BLUE is another hybrid raised by the same firm; the leaves are larger than those of *C. X burkwoodii*, and more glossy green; the flower trusses are larger and of a paler blue shade. (A.M. 1929.)

25. *Lonicera Nitida*, an excellent evergreen for a hedge, particularly in a warm district

26. *Daphne Retusa*, a May-blooming evergreen shrub.

27. *Pyracantha coccinea lolandii*

28. *Magnolia grandiflora*

Both shrubs are excellent on walls in colder districts.

*C. papillosus* (the leaves have wart-like growths: papillae). A tender species discovered by David Douglas in 1833 in California. A lovely blue evergreen shrub, which is at its best in early summer; the deep blue flowers stand out well against the shining green leaves, and the blue and the green are admirably displayed on a wall, where the shrub will reach a height of 12 feet or more. Wall protection is certainly necessary in most inland gardens. The finest specimens I have seen were in gardens in the Isle of Wight.

*C. rigidus* is also one of the tender species, perhaps the most tender and perhaps the most beautiful of the evergreen kinds. It is best treated as a wall shrub; a wall facing west or south-west preferably, and there it will reach a height of 10 feet or more. It has stiff, downy branches covered with closely-packed small leaves ($\frac{1}{2}$ inch long), dark glossy green above and greyish and downy beneath. The dark purplish-blue flowers, crowded together on long shoots, are at their best in May.

The shrub is really too tender even for walls in the London area, and needs the warm climate of Cornwall or the Isle of Wight, if it is to survive.

Like various kinds of *Ceanothus*, the plant is not long-lived; it is wise therefore to take cuttings and have a supply of young plants for stock.

The species is a native of the coastal regions of Central and Southern California and of Monterey; it was introduced into Britain in 1847.

The white- and the pink-flowered *Ceanothus* are less popular with shrub-lovers and not so frequently seen in our gardens.

*C. incanus* is a thorny spreading shrub with creamy-white flowers which come in late spring.

*Ceanothus* need loamy, well-drained soils containing peat or leaf-mould; most gardeners who grow them state 'Soil: light and ordinary.'

Cuttings are taken during July and August and put in sandy soil in gentle heat. Most of the *Ceanothus* obtainable from nurseries cost about 12*s*. 6*d*. a plant.

*Choisya ternata* (having 3 parts, referring to the 3 leaflets of the compound leaf). This is the Mexican Orange Blossom, a fragrant, white-flowered shrub, which sometimes blooms in

December during a mild spell. Normally it blooms in April and May. The leaflets are ovalish, about 1½ to 3 inches long, and of a cool, pleasant green colour. The flowers (rather like those of the Orange tree) smell faintly of Hawthorne and are much appreciated when they bloom near the house; and often one finds this evergreen planted near a wall, under a window. Yet it is perfectly hardy (except in cold northern districts, where it needs a wall); it is one of the few Mexican shrubs that flourish in gardens near London.

*Cistus*, Rock-roses, are well known to most people in the south of England. In the north they are seldom if ever seen; one or perhaps two might survive the cold there: *Cistus laurifolius* and *C. corbariensis* are the hardiest and could be tried in a reasonably sheltered spot. However, the bush Rock-roses are essentially shrubs for the warm south where they are very popular with gardeners. *C. X purpureus* has already been mentioned (Chapter 2, page 43); it is one of the most striking of all flowering evergreen shrubs and easiest to grow – in the right district and the right place.

The plant grows quickly then into a rounded bush about 3 feet high, with sticky dull green narrow leaves (2 inches long), which in the flowering period, from noon till evening are almost hidden by the open single rose-like blooms (3 inches across) of a rose-red colour and blotched with deep crimson. The 'rock-roses' are probably the most evanescent of all flowers, but new buds open successively every day over a period of several weeks and provide a continuous show.

The plant is considered to be a hybrid between *C. villosus* and *C. ladaniferous* or a form of this species, with a deep red blotch at the base of the petals. Both species are natives of the Mediterranean region.

I have grown *C. X purpureus* in my garden but it never lives more than a couple of years: it quickly succumbs to frost. It is a wise precaution to take cuttings every August of your plant (wherever you live) so that you can always have a supply of new plants – in fact with *C. X purpureus* it is essential. (Choose unflowered shoots 4 inches long with a heel, and insert them in sandy soil in pots and keep them under glass, well-shaded from the sun, till they root. Plant them out the following June.) A plant costs about 10*s*.

*C. X corbariensis*. This hybrid, like many hybrids, is hardier than the parent plants; it is probably the hardiest of all the Cistus tribe. The flowers are white and small (1½ inches across), pink-tinted in the bud, the petals stained yellow at the base. The shrub is about 3 feet high and, like all the *Cistus*, revels in hot dry sandy soils and full sun. It is completely hardy but often doesn't live long in rich ground.

*C. X cyprius* is another hardy hybrid; it is said to have originated in Cyprus, and is a tall shrub, up to about 8 feet high in the south; completely hardy in our gardens and, according to Bean: 'The most beautiful of all the Cistuses we can grow out-of-doors.'

The flowers, carried in clusters of from 3 to 6 on a long stalk, are 3 inches across, white with a conspicuous crimson spot at the base of each petal.

The hardiest of all these lovely evergreen shrubs is *C. laurifolius*, which is a native of South-west Europe and the Mediterranean region. The leaves are dark green, and the flowers 3 inches across and pure white. They are at their best in mid-summer. The shrub (about 6 feet tall) is used for covering hot dry slopes, where few other evergreens would grow. The stems and the leaves during hot weather give off a pleasant incense-like smell.

A dwarf *Cistus*, excellent for massing in a large garden, or for growing as a single shrub in a rockery, is *C. X loreti*. (In many catalogues it will be found under the name of *C. lusitanicus*; of which species it is a variety or form; it was found growing wild in the south of France and given the hybrid name by Rouy and Foucaud in their FLORE DE FRANCE).

It is a bush about 18 inches tall; its leaves are narrow, a dull dark green; its flowers white with a crimson blotch. The plant is hardy enough for any gardens around London.

Most of the *Cistus* have white flowers and are less liked by gardeners than the reddish-purple, or pink kinds. Unfortunately there are only a few of these: *C. X purpureus*, the best of them, is decidedly tender.

*C. X pulverulentus* has vivid rose-pink flowers and greyish-green hairy leaves. It makes a compact shrub about 3 feet high; it needs a hot sunny position and is no good in many gardens. (Cuttings should be taken every summer so that a stock is always available; keep the new plants in 5-inch pots and sink these in the garden during the summer, if you do not plant them out.) (*pulverulentus* means as though dusted with powder and probably refers to the hairiness of the leaves.)

*C. X Silver Pink* was raised in Hillier's Nursery at Winchester, Hants., and is the hardiest of the pink or so-called red *Cistus*. The flowers are a good clear silvery-pink and stand out well against the dark green leaves; they are a grey-green beneath; narrow, about 3 inches long. The plant makes a neat bushy shrub about 2 feet high. It received an A.M. in 1919. The shrub costs about 10*s*. – which is the average price of the *Cistus*.

*C. X skanbergii*. This is a rare natural hybrid found wild in Greece; it has small pale pink flowers and attractive dark green foliage. The plant is about the same height as *C. X Silver Pink*.

A red *Cistus* recommended by many growers is the species *C. crispus*, a native of South-west Europe and North Africa, and regarded as one of the hardiest. Actually it is only moderately hardy but it is certainly worth a trial in a sheltered spot for the sake of the purple-red flowers – these are about 1½ inches across. Cuttings should be taken in July.

*Cistus* should be planted while the soil is still summer warm: September is ideal; if not then, they should be put out in late May. Once the shrubs are established, they cannot be transplanted.

*Elaeagnus* contain several evergreen shrubs which prosper in any inland gardens and like the deciduous members of the family do best in ordinary garden soils which are not too rich in humus. They are perfectly hardy and good wind resisters. They haven't much floral beauty; the flowers are small and white or silvery-white, funnel-shaped (Fuchsia-like), and fragrant.

*Elaeagnus glabra* (smooth, hairless) is sometimes trained up a wall and then grows very tall. We mostly grow it as a shrub in the open garden, however, and in time it makes a tallish, rambling plant (10 feet or more high), with narrowish leaves (the underside smooth, with a metallic sheen) and small fragrant flowers which come in late autumn. The species is a native of China and Japan.

*E. macrophylla* (large – or broad-leaved). This is one of the finest of the evergreen species, having ovalish leaves, the largest 4½ inches long, of a delightful silvery colour in their young state. The flowers, like a Fuchsia, are fragrant and come in late autumn, at a time when there are few others to be seen. It makes a good-sized shrub up to 12 feet tall and is usually wider than that.

The plant was introduced into England in 1879 and is a native of Japan and Korea.

*E. pungens* (ending in a sharp point; probably referring to the spiny character of the plant). This is another tallish species, up to 15 feet in height; a vigorous shrub, with ovalish leaves and small fragrant white flowers in autumn; the scent is faintly reminiscent of the exotic Gardenia.

The plant has produced several most attractive varieties, viz.

Var. DICKSONI, with leaves marked with golden-yellow. A very attractive foliage shrub in winter.

Var. REFLEXA (considered to be a hybrid between *E. glabra* and *E. pungens*). It has long branches only slightly spiny; and leaves, shining green above and reddish-brown and scaly beneath. Var. AUREO-VARIEGATA is a special favourite with gardeners and has large leaves with a big patch of deep yellow in the centre. This variety is most decorative in the winter and vies with any of the variegated evergreens we grow.

*Elaeagnus* are sometimes called Oleasters or Wild Olives; though at one time the name Oleaster was reserved for the deciduous species *E. angustifolia*.

*Elaeagnus* can be obtained from any good nursery. Var. AUREO-VARIEGATA costs about 15*s*.

*Escallonia*, with the exception of one species, are all evergreen, and are very well known to most gardeners in the south of England. In many public gardens along the south coast you will see these evergreen shrubs in bloom during late summer and the autumn and often associated with the hardy *Fuchsia magellanica* Var. RICCARTONII. Escallonia are quoted in the O.E.D. viz. 'Looking out on a summer sea from terraces lined with Laurel, fuchsia and escallonia.'

These shrubs do best near the sea and are much less common farther north; there they are grown against a wall to shelter them during severe frosty spells.

Most of them are from Chile and the hot regions of South

America and in England need the warm sea air during the bad winter weather. They thrive in any ordinary loamy soil and are easy to propagate. (Cuttings taken in August root quickly in a closed frame.)

*Escallonia* cross-breed easily and have produced some fine hybrid forms which on the whole are hardier and more vigorous than the parent plants.

The 'Donard Hybrids' from Co. Down are the best I've seen.

DONARD BRILLIANCE has racemes or clusters of rich rose-red flowers and arching branches – a good specimen shrub for a warm sunny place.

DONARD GEM is a pink-flowered sweetly scented variety and likewise an excellent specimen shrub for a warm garden.

*Escallonia* stand up well to wind in coastal districts and some make good hedges or screens up to 6 feet or more in height.

*E. macrantha*, from the island of Chiloe (off the coast of Chile) is the species usually favoured by gardeners for hedges. Its leaves, ovalish (the largest 3 inches long), are toothed and of an attractive dark, shining green. The flowers, which begin blooming in June and continue till autumn, are a charming bright rose-red and about ½ inch long. They come in panicles, usually 2 to 4 inches long.

The handsomest of all the species is *E. montevidensis*, found in South Brazil and near Mount Video in Uruguay. It needs wall protection in Britain unless it grows in a warm seaside garden. The flowers, pure white and fragrant, come in long terminal panicles or clusters in summer and autumn. The leaves, small and ovalish in shape, are of a bright green colour. This shrub sometimes reaches a height of 10 feet on a wall; in its habitat it is much bigger and becomes tree-like.

The hybrid *E. X exoniensis* (*E. pterocladon X E. rubra*) was raised in the nursery of Messrs. Veitch in Exeter and has white or rose-tinted flowers, which bloom from June to October. It is a vigorous shrub reaching a height of 12 feet or more. It was given an A.M. in 1891 and is the best Escallonia for gardens near London. (*Escallonia* cost about half a guinea each.)

*Hypericum calycinum*, the Rose of Sharon is a sub-shrub or under shrub – a plant woody except at the tips of the branches, which die back in the winter. In some districts it remains green all through the year. It is a dwarf shrubby plant known to everybody, a rampant spreader, which used to be grown in many gardens where there was room for it. It quickly overruns everything (rather difficult to eradicate, once it gets a hold), and for that reason perhaps is not often grown nowadays. The lovely open yellow flowers, full of stamens, are well known. The plant will grow practically anywhere: in sun or shade; it thrives under trees and in the large wild garden could be associated with the Holly-leaf Mahonia. (Plants can be bought by the dozen from many nurseries – cost 39*s*. for twelve.) The name *calycinum* means having a conspicuous calyx – this is the outer whorl of floral leaves, those surrounding the flower, and usually green in colour.

*Kalmia latifolia* (broad leaf). This evergreen shrub is sometimes vaguely described as 'a good substitute for a *Rhododendron*.' This could mean that it would grow where a *Rhododendron* would be a failure. This particular *Kalmia* is well known and the most popular of the half a dozen or so species obtainable. But it is not at all amenable to general cultivation and is possibly quite rare in our gardens. Which is a pity, since it is as lovely as any of the small-flowered Rhododendrons we grow. The astonishing thing to many gardeners is that the shrub is found wild anywhere – it looks so much a product of the nurseries. Its clusters of small deep rose-pink flowers (described as 'Icing-sugar pink, and resembling it') stand out well against the leathery, deep glossy green leaves, which are quite small. In gardens it usually reaches a height of 5 feet – often less in many gardens. In its habitat (Eastern North America), though, some shrubs are as much as 30 feet tall. Although this *Kalmia* is so well known and so widely advertised, it is among the most intractable of flowering shrubs. It must have a lime-free, peaty soil, and never be without moisture; it prospers only in warm southern gardens (farther north it doesn't give much of a show); like the following species of *Lonicera*, it makes a good sea-side shrub. One of the popular names of *Kalmia latifolia* is the Mountain Laurel; another the Calico Bush.

*Lonicera nitida* is a very ordinary-looking shrub, though more interesting than the Privet, the foliage being neater and daintier. Like the Privet, it is used for hedging and has become one of the most popular of hedging plants. It responds well to clipping and grows quickly. The shrub is very well known and widely planted. It grows stronger and better, however, in the warmest parts of Britain. One never associates it with the Honeysuckle family (*Lonicera*), and its flowers are very small, creamy-white, slightly fragrant, and not often seen on the plants when they are regularly pruned back. It thrives in any ordinary loam, and occasionally in sea-side gardens will be seen growing as a single specimen shrub, sometimes 10 feet tall or taller.

Rosemary, like Lavender (to which it is related) and Lavender Cotton (*Santolina*), is one of our old-world garden plants – introduced here, it is said, about the same time as these plants, which was the middle of the 16th century. It is less hardy than they, and does best in the south. Old plants are specially vulnerable, the young ones seemingly tolerating several degrees of frost.

In the south it makes a charming low evergreen hedge, although rather untidy, and in May is, in a sunny place, covered with uncommonly beautiful steel-blue flowers.

The Common Rosemary (*Rosmarinus officinalis*) is easily raised by cuttings. The plant needs a lightish loamy soil, well drained, and is a failure in heavy clay, which is always cold and damp through the winter weather.

Pruning and shaping should be done immediately the shrubs have finished flowering, so that the new shoots can grow strong and tall before the autumn.

The leaves, linear (narrow like the Yew leaf), have a smell reminiscent of nutmeg; they are used to flavour meat (mutton especially); and probably no other shrub we grow has so many uses, culinary and medicinal – it would need a chapter to enumerate and describe adequately all its virtues. It is well named *officinalis*, which means 'sold in shops:' used of medicinal and other plants.

Rosemary and its varieties are seldom planted in our gardens nowadays. There is a curiously attractive variety called Var. ALBUS, which I have never seen grown in gardens in this country but it is common in Italy.

Plant Rosemary in May when possible or in September, when the soil is warm.

*Veronica*, like *Escallonia*, are best suited to our warm sea-side gardens and live longer and flower most profusely in southern maritime districts. The shrubs are common enough there and will be found in many parts of the country. They thrive in any good ordinary light loamy soil.

Where you can grow *Ceanothus* successfully, you will also succeed with the best of the *Veronica* – the generic name *Hebe* by the way is used in some catalogues, *Veronica* being reserved for the herbaceous kinds.

The shrubs are natives of New Zealand, and the hardiest of the species and the hybrid forms are quite suitable for growing in many of our inland gardens.

*Veronica anomala* is one of the hardiest and most successful. It makes a fairly erect bush from 3 to 5 feet tall, with white or pale pink flowers which come in a cluster of spikes at the end of the shoots during the summer. The leaves are ovalish and pointed, about ½ inch long and a dark shining green colour.

As this species is inclined to become lanky with age, gardeners who grow it take cuttings every so often to provide them with fresh stock. Young-wood shoots are best and should be taken in summer.

Another hardy species is *Veronica brachysiphon* introduced from New Zealand in 1868. It is a July bloomer and charming when covered with its small white flowers. When fully grown, it is a wide spreading rounded bush of dense habit, 6 feet or more high. The leaves are a dark dull green, small and densely arranged in 4 even rows up the stems.

This is one of the most attractive of all the hardy Veronicas, and is often planted as an isolated specimen on a lawn. No better place could be found for it. Its rounded shape and masses of flowers are seen to best advantage there.

*V. darwiniana*. This species is known as Darwin's Speedwell (Speedwell being the popular name of the plants). It makes a neat shrub up to 3 feet high covered with white flowers; the leaves are narrowly lance-shaped and of an attractive glaucous-blue colour. The plant is a native of both the main islands of New Zealand, where it grows taller and bigger than it does in our gardens. It is one of the hardiest.

*V. speciosa* (beautiful; showy) has been called the loveliest of all the Veronicas. It is found wild in the North Island of New Zealand, but it is doubtful whether the shrub is now in cultivation anywhere. Botanists seem to think not. It is a spreading shrub up to 5 feet high, with glossy green leaves, ovalish, 2 to 4 inches long and racemes of reddish-purple flowers, which make it the showiest of all the Veronicas.

The species has been crossed with others and produced some magnificent garden varieties which flourish in our warmest southern gardens. These shrubs are the brightest-coloured of all the Veronicas found in Britain; and the one called Var. AUTUMN GLORY is the best known and much hardier than the others. It is 2 to 3 feet high and carries masses of deep violet-blue flowers in short racemes all through the late summer and autumn, in fact until the frosts come. It is well worth planting for a late show of flowers. Good specimens may be bought from any shrub nursery for 8*s*. 6*d*. each.

*V. elliptica* is the best known and most widely planted of the shrub Veronicas in our coastal gardens. (A native of New Zealand, Chile, Tierra del Fuego and the Falkland Islands; first introduced as long ago as 1776; then it was re-introduced by Mr. Clarence Elliott in 1909.) It is a favourite shrub with gardeners in the south for hedging. Occasionally you will see it grown as a specimen shrub or tree, up to 20 feet tall; more often it is a shrub from 3 to 5 feet, and singularly attractive when in full bloom. The flowers are white, fragrant and the largest of those of the shrubby species. The leaves are oval, about 1 inch long and ½ inch wide. The plant is easily increased by young wood cuttings (the cheapest way of obtaining a good quantity for hedges). A good specimen can be obtained for about 8*s*. 6*d*.

*Yucca* are described as evergreen trees and shrubs, natives of the Southern United States, Mexico, and Central America. Some, like *Yucca glauca*, are very hardy but need a warm sunny climate if they are to give a good show of flowers. They are ideal plants for the semi-tropical garden and best suited to wide spaces and large borders. They look out of place in a small garden. Yuccas are well known to most gardeners but not widely grown in this country.

*Y. filamentosa* (thread-like, referring to the curly, thread-like filaments on the margins of the leaves). This is one of the dwarfer species; it has erect panicles of yellowish-white, pendulous lily-like flowers in August; the panicles are usually

3 to 6 feet high. The leaves are characteristic of the *Yucca*, tropical-looking, long, narrow, stiff and sometimes spine-tipped. A handsome, stately plant for the formal garden.

*Y. flaccida* (weak, feeble, probably in reference to the leaves, the terminal parts being bent downwards and less sword-like and sharp than many). It is allied to *Y. filamentosa*; the chief differences are in the leaves, and the flowers which come in rather shorter panicles. Both species are natives of the south-eastern United States. Plants cost about 12*s*. 6*d*. each.

*Y. glauca* (having grey or bluish-green leaves). This species has the same habitat as the two above, but it does not flower very freely. The flowers, about 3 inches long, are a greenish-white (not so striking as the pure white) and are carried in erect racemes 3 to 4 feet high.

*Y. gloriosa* has long been known in our gardens but needs plenty of room to make a good show – a single *Yucca* anywhere looks odd. Like all the plants, it is best massed; and the best place for them is a sunny border where the soil is a lightish, sandy loam, well drained. (*Yucca* make a magnificent show when they are interplanted with the contrasting soft, velvety, silver-white foliage-plant, *Senecio cineraria*, familiarly known as 'Dusty Miller'.) The name *gloriosa* means glorious, full of glory, probably referring to the tall spikes of flowers when in bloom. They stand up conspicuously above the clusters of stiff, straight, spine-tipped leaves, which are glaucous green.

*Y. recurvifolia* (curved backwards, referring to the leaves). This plant often reaches a height of 6 feet in our warm southern counties. The leaves are from 2 to 3 feet long, 1½ to 2½ inches wide, tapered to a spiny point; the upper ones are stiff and sword-like; the lower ones much recurved. The flowers, creamy-white, 2 to 3 inches wide, lily-like, and pendulous, come in erect panicles 3 to 5 feet tall. A grand, imposing plant which gives an exotic look to gardens where it can be massed.

Most of the *Yucca* bloom in late summer or early autumn and are valuable ornamentals on that account. Formal bedding-plants such as the *Senecio* mentioned above are about the best to grow with them.

*Y. gloriosa* was known in this country in the 16th century and mentioned by Gerard in his Herbal and grown by him in his garden at Holborn.

The common names of the *Yucca* are Adam's Needle, Spanish Bayonet and Spanish Dagger.

2

*Abelia floribunda* is a good evergreen shrub to start this section with. It is both rare and tender – it is too tender for the open garden in most districts, and even in the south it thrives better and flowers more freely when planted against a wall. Near London it is often very short lived and a failure even when grown on a wall, unless it is given protection through frosty weather. This lovely evergreen (up to 20 feet high on south walls in our warmest maritime counties) has small ovalish glossy green leaves, and charming funnel-shaped, crimson-lake, pendulous flowers in June. The plant has a festive look and is wonderfully decorative grown under glass. It is a native of mountainous regions of the southern Pacific State of Oaxaca in Mexico. It grows there at an altitude of 10,000 feet and makes a shrub from 6 to 10 feet tall.

*Acacia dealbata* (the Mimosa of the south of France) was mentioned in the chapter on evergreen trees (page 50). It is too tender for any gardens outside Cornwall or other counties with a similar climate. It is a rare evergreen, and one hardly expects to see it growing anywhere in this country. In Italy and the south of France it is common enough; and at Tresco Abbey in the Scilly Isles as many as 60 species of *Acacia* are grown and flourish luxuriantly. Acacias need full sun, and do best in peaty loamy soils. About a dozen different kinds are cultivated in our islands – in warm maritime gardens; but they are very rare.

*A. baileyana*, known as Bailey's Mimosa, is one of the loveliest of them (it received an A.M. in 1927). It makes a charming small evergreen tree, with vivid bluish-white foliage and a profusion of rich yellow blossom – tiny ball-shaped flowers, ¼ inch wide. It is one of the most striking of the Wattles of Australia and prized by growers for its wonderful foliage.

*Acradenia frankliniae* from Western Tasmania is doubtless known only to a few gardeners. It is usually grown in a cool greenhouse, where it makes an attractive evergreen shrub, with dark green trifoliate leaves and clusters (2 inches across) of white flowers. It needs the warmest of our seaside gardens, if it is to grow well and flower freely. In gardens on the Atlantic seaboard of Southern Ireland it makes a rounded shrub 6 feet or more high. In gardens of the French Riviera it reaches a height of 10 feet or more. Hillier of Winchester, Hampshire, can supply the shrub – it costs 21*s*.

*Andromeda poliofolia*, known to growers of the shrub as the Bog Rosemary. A dwarf evergreen about 18 inches high, with hard-textured Yew-like leaves and clusters of small bell-shaped, pink flowers, which come in May and later through the summer. It needs a moist, cool, peaty soil. Useless in dry districts, such as the Thames Valley in summer. Made-up beds of peat are not always a success. It is a native of peat bogs in North Europe; and found in Yorkshire and other parts of Britain.

*Arbutus andrachne* is the Grecian 'Strawberry Tree'. A native of South-eastern Europe and especially abundant in the Eastern Mediterranean region. In the wild it attains a height of about 40 feet; but in our gardens, where, by the way, it is rarely grown, it is seldom more than a good-sized shrub. It is decidedly on the tender side around London. I like its reddish-brown bark. The 'strawberry' fruits are smooth and smaller than those of *Arbutus unedo* (see page 47).

*A. X andrachnoides* (*A. andrachne X A. unedo*) is a natural hybrid which originated in Greece, where both its parents grow. It is hardier than *A. andrachne*; similarly its great attraction is its beautiful cinnamon-red bark. The shrub deserves to be much more widely grown. It will thrive where lime is present in the soil, as will the other kinds; they all like a good depth of rich, moist loam.

*Arctostaphylos* are rarely grown in our gardens. Actually I've never seen them outside Botanical collections. They like peaty, lime-free soil, such as Rhododendrons require, and they belong to the *Ericaceae* Family which includes these shrubs (and Azaleas), Heathers, Andromedas and many peat-loving plants. They need more sun however than Rhododendrons and Azaleas; in fact one of the choicest, *A. manzanita*, needs full sun and a moist peaty soil; and according to people who grow it, it is among the most intractable of all shrubs – well nigh impossible to establish in most gardens. It is an attractive evergreen but not as showy as the hybrid Rhododendrons and the Camellia varieties. It is a native of California, with ovalish leaves about 3 inches long and 2 inches wide, thick and leathery; and small pink flowers, bell-shaped, which bloom from February to April.

More amenable to cultivation in our gardens is *A. uva-ursi* (the Red Bearberry), a native plant from the mountainous parts of northern England and Scotland; it is also found in Central Europe. It is a charming evergreen trailing plant carrying pink flowers in small drooping clusters from April to June. An excellent ground-cover to set among tall Rhododendrons.

The Californian Manzanita seems difficult to get; *A. uva-ursi* may be bought from most shrub nurseries for about 12*s*. 6*d*.

*Azara* are too tender for most of our gardens. *A. microphylla* is the hardiest; in the warmer south-western regions of these islands it will reach a height of 30 feet or more; and with its small glossy green leaves and frond-like arrangement of the branches, is a fine ornamental evergreen for the open garden or for training against a wall. The small, vanilla-scented flowers, which come in March make the plant doubly valuable at this time of the year. It doesn't live long unfortunately in the open garden in districts around London.

*A. petiolaris* is, I think, the most decorative of the half a dozen or so species available; but it is the most tender and only really suitable for cool greenhouse culture outside south-western counties of England. It has handsome Holly-like leaves and deliciously fragrant yellow flowers in small clusters in spring.

*Azara* can be bought from most shrub specialists, and cost about 15*s*. 6*d*. each.

*Baccharis patagonica* is a native of Patogonia where it is known as the Groundsel Tree. It is very rarely seen in our gardens; and is here never much more than a shrub (of open but stiff habit), about 8 feet tall. The small evergreen dark polished leaves are its chief attraction; the flowers, which come in small heads, yellowish-white, are by no means striking. It succeeds in any loamy soil and would be a useful background shrub for some of the smaller hybrid Rhododendrons.

*Banksia* are tender evergreen shrubs and rarely seen outside a cool greenhouse in this country. They are natives of Australia and known sometimes as the Australian Honeysuckle. *B. integrifolia* succeeds on warm south walls in districts where the Mimosa thrives; but the few good specimens I have seen have been grown under glass. It is chiefly for its ornamental foliage that the plant is valued – the leaves are leathery, olive-green above and white beneath; the flowers yellow. This evergreen shrub can be got from most shrub specialists.

*Beschorneria yuccoides* is a Yucca-like plant from Mexico, and outside needs to be grown near a south wall – not too close, however, to spoil the symmetry of its Yucca-like rosette of leaves, 2 feet long, 3 inches wide and sharply pointed. The flower stems reach a height of 4 to 6 feet and carry drooping racemes of green flowers (rather like a Fuchsia's) with red bracts. The stems are also reddish; and the contrast between the green and the red gives a pleasing effect in summer. The plant is not hardy enough for gardens in the London area.

*Bowkeria gerrardiana* is one of the few evergreen shrubs from South Africa which can be grown in the open in our southernmost districts. It succeeds and flowers well in the Isle of Wight; but elsewhere needs a cold greenhouse. In August it has large, white Calceolaria-like flowers; very beautiful; these stand out well against the dull green leaves, which are stalkless, on branches or stems covered with fine grey hairs. Where a suitable spot can be found for it, it will make a shrub up to 10 feet high.

*Brachyglottis repanda*, a shrub or small tree up to 20 feet tall in the North and South Islands of New Zealand. There it flowers in August (in Britain much earlier); it is used in places like Cornwall and South Devon to create tropical effects in large gardens. It is useless in inland districts farther north. A magnificent evergreen foliage-plant (where it can be grown): the large ovalish leaves (the largest 12 inches long), glossy green, tinged with purple above, and white beneath, are very striking. The flower-heads, small and greenish-white, are fragrant and come in panicles as much as a foot long. But it is as a foliage-shrub that it is prized by gardeners who can grow it.

*Bryanthus musciformis* is a rare Heather-like shrub, with larger leaves and flowers, however, than those of the Heather. The leaves, linear, $\frac{1}{4}$ inch long, contrast well with the rosy-pink flowers ($\frac{1}{4}$ inch wide), which are carried in threes or more on slender, erect stems. It needs lime-free peaty soils, as does some of the Heathers, and would make an interesting prostrate shrublet for the rockery. It is a collector's plant and a rarity.

*Bupleurum fruticosa*, a native of Southern Europe and the Mediterranean Region, is grown chiefly for its handsome bluish-green leaves; but it needs a warm maritime district or a garden in the south-west if it is to survive our bad winters. Near London it must have the protection of a wall; at Kew, for instance, it has made a fine shrub, 8 feet or more high, on a wall. The flowers, a pretty shade of yellow, come in terminal clusters 3 inches across, and stand out well against the bluish-green foliage. It blooms from July to September and will be seen in some sea-side gardens, growing high up on cliffs, and in chalky soil, a place for which it is well adapted.

*Bursaria spinosa* is a native of New South Wales and Tasmania and a tender evergreen shrub 8 feet tall in this country – in places where it can be grown successfully. Warm sea-side gardens in the south are the best. On walls in these places it grows taller and during August it is singularly attractive when covered with its tiny white fragrant flowers. The leaves are small and dainty; some of the branches are spiny; others unarmed. Late in autumn the shrub bears striking pouch-like red fruits.

*Calceolaria* are best known by the greenhouse and bedding-out kinds, plants which are admired by all. Chiefly for their delightful pouch-like flowers. *Calceolaria integrifolia* is suitable for gardens in the south-western counties; but elsewhere it must be protected against frost and cold winds. It is best not to attempt to grow it, if you cannot give it a position against a warm south or west wall. It makes an erect bushy plant, 4 feet tall, with sage-like leaves, dull green above and greyish and downy beneath. The flowers, bright yellow, charmingly 'pouched,' are about ½ inch wide and are freely borne during the summer months. This beautiful evergreen shrub, a native of Chile, was introduced into Britain in 1822. Most gardeners want to grow it. As well as planting it at the foot of a wall, those who try it, should cover it up with some sort of protective material when the cold weather arrives. It needs a well-drained, lightish loamy soil. A specimen costs about 15*s*. 6*d*.

*Carpenteria californica* is a beautiful seaside shrub with pure white fragrant, Anemone-shaped flowers (3 inches wide) and narrow leaves, rich green above and greyish beneath. They are an excellent foil to the flowers, which resemble those of

29. *Fatsia Japonica*, a handsome evergreen foliage plant.

30. *Garrya Elliptica*—noted for its long catkins in mid-winter.

31. *Gaultheria Procumbens*, a charming dwarf evergreen with red berries.

32. *Pernettya Muconata*, the showiest of all dwarf berrying evergreens.

33. *Phlomis fruticosa*, a partially tender silver-grey evergreen shrub with yellow flowers.

34. *Viburnum x Burkwoodii*, a lovely early-blooming evergreen shrub for town gardens.

our common Philadelphus (Mock Orange). The shrub is known as the Californian Mock Orange; it is much more striking than our deciduous plant. It needs the protection of a wall in inland gardens and reaches a height of 12 feet or more in favourable districts. Unfortunately it is short-lived in town and city gardens, even in the south; a clear, sunny atmosphere is as important to it as a warm equable climate. It should be planted in May in a well-drained leafy, loamy soil. The shrub does not appear to be very long-lived; it is best raised from seed.

*Cassinia fulvida*, a shrub I have grown here in Bucks., for many years, is not listed in any current catalogues I possess. It isn't seen in many gardens; but it is completely hardy and although the flowers are dull, untidy-looking, unattractive, the foliage, golden coloured, is very beautiful, especially in spring. It is essentially a foliage-plant; the flowers are worthless. The shrub is a native of New Zealand, where it is known as the Golden Heather; and in our gardens usually reaches a height of 3 to 4 feet; it needs a loamy, leafy soil and shelter from cold winds. The very small leaves, crowded on the slender stems, are green above and golden-yellow beneath. The plant is at its best in early spring, when the new golden-yellow shoots appear.

*Cassiope* are dwarf shrubs which belong to the *Ericaceae* family and revel in cool, moist, peaty soils. They have Heather-like leaves and flowers. Whereas most of the evergreens I have described in this Section need a warm, sunny, sheltered situation in a southern garden, *Cassiope* need just the opposite – a cold, moist place, such as they would get in a high mountainous region, where they would lie under snow all the winter. They probably do better in Iceland than in England. I don't know of any gardens around London where they are a success. One of the loveliest is *Cassiope lycopodioides* from the mountains of Japan. It is best in a bed of cool peat in a place facing north, where the sun doesn't come till late evening. It has dense, prostrate overlapping stems which ultimately form a mat-like plant 2 to 3 feet wide; the white Lily-of-the valley-like flowers come in May and June.

*Cassiope tetragona* (sometimes called *Andromeda*; see page 157 for a description of this plant). This species from the cold arctic regions makes a dwarf evergreen shrublet 4 to 10 inches high, with tiny leaves and flowers similar to those of the above species but the flowers are tinged with red and lovely in April and May against the deep green foliage.

*Cornus* (Dogwoods) are common enough; but the evergreen species *C. oblonga* is very rarely seen in our gardens. (Apart from this species and *C. capitata* – sometimes semi-evergreen –, the species listed in catalogues are all leaf-shedding kinds.) Marchant describes *C. oblonga*, a native of Northern India and China, as 'An exceedingly rare and attractive evergreen growing 8 feet or more high, for gardens in the south and west . . . ' In its habitat it makes a fine shrub or small tree up to 20 feet tall; in cultivation it is about half that size. The leaves are ovalish, the largest 5 inches long, a dark glossy green above and greyish beneath. The flowers, delightfully fragrant, and creamy-white, come in panicles at the end of the stems. It is a lovely evergreen shrub but not worth troubling with in our inland gardens. Nor is the other, *C. capitata*, which is sometimes semi-evergreen. Of the two, *C. capitata*, I think, is the finer. It is also a native of Northern India and China. There it is a bushy shrub 40 feet high and often twice as much in width.

The best places for it in these islands are the warm gardens of Cornwall and those on the Atlantic seaboard of south-west Ireland. There in June large specimens will be seen covered with glorious pale yellow flowers (really bracts, 2 inches long and an inch wide, which surround the tiny, genuine flowers). The leaves, evergreen in warm districts, are leathery, ovalish, the largest 5 inches long, and of an attractive dull grey-green colour.

Many of the evergreens described in this section are natives of New Zealand. *Corokia* belong there and are moderately-tall shrubs suitable only for our warm south-western counties – with the possible exception of *C. virgata*, which catalogues describe as 'hardy'. Marchant says: 'This *very hardy* shrub has twiggy branches, and is of graceful habit . . . ' It was given an A.M. in 1934; it is not very hardy in gardens near London; for it mostly disappears during a severe winter, its slender twigs being cut to the ground. They shoot up again in the following spring, however; but the shrub is really safer against a warm south wall in this district and certainly in gardens farther north. It is the most floriferous and the freest berrying of the few species known. The flowers are yellow, small and star-shaped (in May); and the berries bright orange in autumn.

The best known is *C. cotoneaster*, called the 'Wire-netting Bush': the branches, thin and rigid, are tortuous and interlaced, forming almost a net-work of white downy growths, which later, as they age, turn blackish. The roundish, curious, spoon-shaped leaves are small, dark green above and white beneath; the flowers, star-shaped (½ inch across) and bright yellow (May and June blooming); the fruits, red and cherry-like in autumn. The shrub reaches a height of 8 feet in warm districts and is suitable only for a wall in our inland gardens.

*Correa* are known as the Australian Fuchsias; the flowers are tubular, pendent, about an inch long and scarlet, white, or pale yellow. The shrubs are often grown in a cool greenhouse, where they make charming ornamental plants for the winter.

*Correa harrisii* succeeds only in warm, sheltered gardens, and grows better and more strongly against a wall. The flowers are a beautiful dark crimson colour.

*C. speciosa* has roundish leaves and tubular primrose-yellow flowers with green reverse; they bloom for best part of the year, and come more free y when the shrub grows near a south or a west wall; in such a spot it will reach a height of 8 feet or more. Var. PULCHELLA, with palest yellow flowers, is particularly useful in the south, blooming practically all the winter. *Correa* need a peaty, loamy soil with an admixture of sand.

*Cortaderia argentea*, the Pampas Grass, is usually classed as an evergreen shrub. It is known to every gardener; but not grown much nowadays. For one thing, it takes up too much room; and during the winter it is often untidy-looking – shabby and something of an eyesore before the new feathery plumes start to grow again. The Pampas Grass likes a lightish ordinary garden loam.

*Cyathodes colensoi* is another New Zealand evergreen and is apparently quite hardy in most of our gardens. It is rarely seen, however; its blue-green foliage covering the prostrate stems which carry attractive white fruits in autumn make it a fine spreading shrublet for planting with Heathers, Rhododendrons and other peat-loving plants. (A.M. 1962).

*C. robusta*, a native of the Chatham Islands (New Zealand)

is rarer and tender. It is a small erect shrub rather resembling a miniature Pine-tree.

*Dacrydium* (closely akin to the Yews) occur mostly in Australasia; but some species are found in Chile, Borneo and the Malay Peninsular. They need peaty, loamy soils. Three or four species may be grown in our warmest seaside gardens, where they will make fine evergreen tallish shrubs or small trees. None is hardy enough for inland gardens in this country.

*D. bidwillii*, from New Zealand, makes a fine evergreen shrub, closely branched, up to 8 feet tall, sometimes taller; depending on the place where it is grown. The leaves on young plants are linear (⅓ inch long); on old plants scale-like, and closely pressed to the stems, like those of the *Cupressus*.

The seeds are like those of the Yew – set in a fleshy fruit (but white in colour: not red).

*D. franklinii* is the Huon Pine of Tasmania, a fine conifer in its natural habitat, where it reaches a height of 100 feet. It has graceful arching branches and attractive Cypress-like foliage.

*Danaë racemosa* (the Alexandrian Laurel) is a native of North Persia and Asia Minor. An excellent shrub for a shady place. The bright green foliage is attractive all through the year; sprays are ideal for cutting and setting among other flowers. It is an elegant small shrub, 2 to 4 feet high, rather Bamboo-like. The flowers are small and greenish-yellow; the berries red and most attractive when borne in quantity. The shrub doesn't fruit freely in many gardens, however. It needs a moist loamy soil, and a shady spot.

The genus *Daphne* is represented in the vast majority of our gardens by the deciduous Mezereum or Mezereon, long known and valued in Britain for its richly scented purplish flowers in February. The evergreen kinds are rare and fairly difficult to establish in the average garden. *D. cneorum* is said to do best in seaside gardens, within reach of the salt air. But if small plants are grown, and put in a permanently moist-leafy loam (they don't mind lime), they will thrive and flower profusely. The leaves are small, narrow and dark green; and the flowers, rose-red (in terminal clusters or heads), are wonderfully fragrant. They bloom in April and May. This shrub is never more than 12 inches high and is a fine trailing evergreen for the rock-garden. Its habitat is Central and Southern Europe.

*D. laureola*, the Spurge Laurel, has the same habitat and is also occasionally found in Britain. It makes a bushy shrub up to 4 feet high, and prospers in moist soils on the heavy side, in semi-shade. Its dark green, shining leaves, thick and firm, are its great attraction; the flowers, sometimes fragrant, sometimes scentless, are small and yellowish-green and come in March.

*D. odora* is the most fragrant of all the Daphnes and probably for that reason often grown in a pot. The flowers are red-purple and are carried in terminal heads; they bloom in mid-winter. The shrub (4 to 6 feet high) is frequently grown near a window so that the rich scent can be enjoyed at all times. Unfortunately the plant is too tender for most inland gardens.

*D. retusa*, a native of Western China, is seldom grown. Marchant says of it: 'This rarity of a difficult genus is one of the easiest to grow.' It reaches a height of about 18 inches and has stiffish branches, with small ovalish dark glossy green leaves, and terminal clusters of fragrant rose-purple flowers. (A.M. 1927.) It is hardy but very rare. (cost is about 15*s.* a plant.)

*Daphniphyllum macropodum* is an evergreen shrub 8 to 12 feet high with ovalish, Laurel-like leaves, dark green above and glaucous beneath. Often the leaf-stalks, mid-ribs, and young wood and red, which adds to the beauty of the plant. The flowers, greenish are small and unattractive. It is quite hardy and succeeds in loamy soils; but is rarely seen – possibly because its flowers are so inconspicuous (many shrubs have foliage just as handsome – Rhododendrons, for example – and also masses of lovely flowers). The shrub, a native of Japan, was introduced into Britain as long ago as 1879.

*Drimys* are akin to the *Magnolia* and were at one time included in that family. They are hardy near the sea and in sheltered inland gardens; but more difficult to establish than the *Magnolia*. *Drimys winteri* and the variety LATIFOLIA are the best known and natives of South America. In the south-west of England *D. winteri* makes a free-growing shrub up to about 20 feet tall, with longish leaves (5 to 10 inches in length), aromatic; and loose clusters of smallish flowers (1 inch wide), ivory-white and fragrant. The shrub resembles a tall evergreen *Magnolia*.

Var. LATIFOLIA has larger leaves and flowers and is a taller-growing shrub – in favourable districts it reaches tree-size. Unfortunately neither is suitable for our gardens inland. *Drimys* need warm loamy soils and are lime-tolerant.

*Embothrium coccineum* is the Fire Bush. It has been described by growers as the most gorgeously coloured of all evergreens that flower in Britain. The flattish clusters of Honeysuckle-like flowers are a fiery scarlet and come in great profusion during May; the foliage, dark glossy green, is a perfect foil to the brilliant scarlet colour. In places where it will grow, the shrub reaches a height of 30 feet and measures as much across. It is very doubtful whether the plant (a native of Chile) will live anywhere outside the warmest regions of these islands – the finest specimens will be found in south Cornwall and south-west Ireland. It needs deep loamy, lime-free soils.

This gorgeous evergreen unfortunately seldom lives more than 20 years; cuttings are therefore always taken or suckers preserved and rooted in pots to provide new stock. (A plant costs about 15*s*.)

*Empetrum nigrum* is a dwarf-growing Heather-like shrub, with spreading, procumbent stems, and small pinkish flowers, which are lovely in March against the dark green foliage. It needs a lime-free soil and is quite hardy but rarely seen in our gardens. The plant is known as the 'Crowberry.'

*Eucryphia* flourish best in districts where the finest of our Rhododendrons grow. They like cool, lime-free peaty soils (though one or two species do well on limy ground) and ample moisture. The flowers are white, and in shape rather resemble those of some beautiful white Rose of Sharon (*Hypericum*, see page 150). *Eucryphia* are all very lovely, but too tender for most gardens. The one I know best (of the half a dozen kinds obtainable) is the hybrid *E. X nymansay*; I have seen it only bush-size; but in warm gardens in the south it grows tall and tree-like. The flowers, pure white, 2½ inches wide, open in August and have lovely, conspicuous yellow stamens. The leaves, compound, are a dark glossy green and beautiful all through the year. It is quite hardy and apparently thrives in ordinary loamy soils. It deserves to be more widely grown. (A plant costs about 20*s*.)

*Fabiana imbricata*, a Heather-like shrub, from Chile, is a fine evergreen (usually 4 feet or more tall) for a warm seaside garden; but is hardly worth growing in low valley districts, especially near London. It needs winter protection there, and seldom then gives much of a show. The branches are crowded with small twigs which are covered with tiny white tubular flowers in June. The plant does best in a light, leafy, well-drained soil.

*Fatsia japonica* is often grown in pots for indoor decoration and erroneously called the Castor Oil Plant. It is well known and valued for its large palmate leaves, deeply lobed at the base. Dark shining green above and paler beneath. It seldom survives a winter outside in this part of Bucks., and is best housed from November to April. In the warm south it attains the height of a large shrub (often 10 to 12 feet), and makes a handsome specimen shrub for a semi-shady place. I have not seen the plant in flower; but in some gardens it gives a good show in early autumn; the panicles of creamy-white flowers are from 12 to 18 inches long. This *Fatsia* is a native of Japan and will thrive in ordinary loamy soils.

*Garrya* are evergreen shrubs (a few tree-like) which are too tender and scarcely decorative enough for the garden. The only exception is *Garrya elliptica*, a native of California and Oregon, which however does better in the south than near London. Here it needs a warm sheltered spot, if it is to produce abundantly its clusters of remarkably fine silvery-grey catkins. These are the plant's chief attraction; they come in late autumn and winter and are doubly welcome at this time of the year. In Cornwall and South Devon the shrub reaches a height of 16 feet and is as much through; the evergreen leaves, ovalish (1½ to 3 inches long), are dark shining green above and grey and woolly beneath. The male plant, with finer, longer catkins, is generally considered a better ornamental shrub than the female. Both need a loamy soil on the light side and full sun. In inland gardens it is best grown near a south wall. *Garrya elliptica* costs 13*s*. 6*d*. a plant.

The difficulty of growing *Gaultheria* is finding a cool semi-shady situation for them. If you have a woodland, you can grow most of those offered by nurseries – unless your garden is in the midlands or farther north, then it will be too cold for these plants. Furthermore they must have a lime-free peaty, loamy soil, such as Rhododendrons and many Heathers need. *Gaultheria* are not found in many gardens. The best known is *G. shallon*, a native of western North America, one of the habitats of the genus (other species come from China, the Himalaya, and Australasia). In cultivation it usually forms a dense thicket of stems (2 to 6 feet high – oftener a low shrub) covered with leathery, ovalish leaves; and in May with tiny pink flowers in racemes; the dark purple fruits come in the autumn and are much relished by game – particularly pheasants.

The shrub does best in thin woodland and is used on large estates as a cover for game. It spreads by means of underground stems.

*G. procumbens* is a favourite dwarf species and, like the above, a native of North America where it is known as the 'Partridge Berry.' It is a creeping evergreen, 2 to 6 inches high, with dark green leaves, pinkish-white flowers in July and August, and bright red berries in autumn. A useful plant for massing among tall-growing Rhododendrons and Azaleas.

*Gordonia axillaris* was first named *Camellia axillaris* (*Gordonia* and *Camellia* are related), and the flower does resemble a single white Camellia. It is creamy-white, 3 to 6 inches wide, with 5 or 6 petals and a centre of numerous stamens and bright yellow anthers. The dark green leathery leaves (the largest about 7 inches long and 3 inches wide) are very handsome and make the plant a valuable evergreen for gardens where it can be grown. Cornwall and south-west Ireland are the best places for it. The flowers come intermittently from November to May. It is a favourite shrub for growing in a cold greenhouse.

*Grevillea alpina*, like the *Gordonia*, is frequently grown in a pot; it is only a success in southern maritime districts. The plant is a native of south Australia, where it is a dwarf bushy rounded shrub. The flowers rather resemble tiny clusters of Honeysuckle and are red at the base, yellow at the top. A charming and most useful little shrub for a rock-garden in the south of England. It is in bloom for best part of the year. (A plant costs about 12*s*. 6*d*.)

*Griselinia littoralis*, another tender New Zealand plant, is soon destroyed by cold in gardens in the Home Counties and anywhere farther north. In warm Cornish gardens, however, it makes a fine, densely-leafy evergreen shrub (sometimes tree-like, up to 25 feet tall), with small yellowish flowers in May. The leaves, leathery and ovalish (the largest 3 inches long), are a refreshing green colour. Many gardeners who can grow it, use it for a hedge.

*Guevina avellana* has been grown in some of our inland gardens, but has always to be covered up during the winter to protect it from cold and frosts. This is a difficult job and sometimes useless, since the cold penetrates the protective material and kills the plant. It is a native of Chile and in warm seaside gardens makes a fine evergreen tree 30 feet tall. The leaflets (of the large leaves) are sharply toothed, ovalish and of a rich, shining green colour. The flowers, with very narrow recurved sepals, are usually whitish in colour and come in long racemes. The plant does best in a semi-shady place.

*Hoheria lyallii* is one of the most handsome of evergreens to come to us from New Zealand. It needs a rich loamy soil in good heart and can only be grown successfully in the warm south. There it soon grows into a fine shrub or small tree, with attractive glaucous leaves, and clusters of fragrant, Cherry-blossom-like flowers in late July. (A.M. 1955.)

*Kalmiopsis leachiana* is very rare in Nature and in danger of becoming extinct. A little evergreen Kalmia-like shrub (6 to 12 inches high) with sugar-pink-coloured Kalmia-blossoms against glossy, light green foliage. It makes an admirable shrublet for a pocket of well-drained peaty soil in the rockery. It is quite hardy but must have the right kind of soil. At the moment the plant is difficult to get and is not priced in any catalogues I possess.

*Laurelia serrata* is known as the 'Chilean Laurel' (it is a native of Chile) and is a fine evergreen shrub or small tree for the warmest parts of Britain. It thrives in and around Winchester, Hampshire. The leaves, leathery and narrow (the largest 5 inches long and 2 inches wide) are a dark, glossy green, and have an aroma reminiscent of the Bay-leaf when crushed or rubbed between the fingers. The plant will reach a height of 15 feet when grown near a wall.

*Ledum*, inhabitants of swampy peat moors of the northern latitudes, are difficult to establish in many gardens. *L. groenlandicum* from North America and Greenland, 2 to 3 feet tall, with narrow leaves and small clusters of white flowers, is the best known and most useful for gardens. It needs a semi-shady spot and blooms from April to June.

*Leptospermum* are evergreen shrubs from New Zealand and not difficult to grow in our warm counties. In cold districts they are scarcely worth troubling with, for they will need protection all through the winter. They have been grown successfully, however, at the foot of south or west walls; though in most gardens walls will no doubt be kept for some more beautiful tender plants.

The best for the average warm, sheltered garden is *Leptospermum scoparium*, a tallish shrub (up to 15 feet in some places), with linear-oblong leaves, ½ inch long, and small white flowers. The varieties are better known perhaps. I single out Var. BOSCAWENII, with pink and white flowers; Var. NANUM, a dwarf (about 1 foot tall) with rose-pink flowers – a lovely plant for the alpine-house; and Var. PROSTRATUM, a creeping shrublet for the rock-garden. *Leptospermum* need well drained peaty soils.

The Myrtle has a strange fascination for people – everybody, it seems, wants to grow it. Maybe it is its association with weddings that appeals to them. The common sort, *Myrtus communis* and more especially the variety TARENTINA are often used in bridal bouquets; the small white flowers are delightfully fragrant, and the leaves small and attractive. In a warm district, near the sea, the flowers come in July in great profusion. The shrub is well worth trying in a sheltered garden (grown on a warm south wall) in inland districts. I have never seen any very healthy specimens, however, in this district, South Bucks. Both plants cost about 12*s*. 6*d*. each.

*Nerium oleander* is far too tender for the vast majority of our gardens. Even in the warmest southern districts of the British Isles, it needs a sheltered spot during the winter months. It is best grown in a pot or a tub and brought indoors about November. It is the 'Oleander' of the East – a mysterious plant, it is said. An eccentric gardener I know grows it, he tells me, because the flowers will poison anybody who eats them! The leaves are leathery in texture, lance-shaped, average length 6 inches (about 1 inch wide) and of a lovely deep green colour. The flowers come in clusters at the tips of the shoots; they are tubular at the base but open out at the top; and are single, semi-double, or double. Var. ALBUM is single, white. Var. LUTEUM PLENUM, sulphur-yellow, double. Var. SPLENDENS, scarlet – a sinister-looking plant when in full bloom!

*Olearia* are the evergreen 'Daisy Bushes' of Australasia; about two dozen species are listed in nurserymen's catalogues; and of these only one, namely *Olearia haastii*, is considered to be generally hardy. It is a native of New Zealand and makes a rounded bushy shrub from 4 to 9 feet tall. It prospers in gardens around London but does not grow so tall there as it does in, say, Devon and Cornwall. Very fine specimens grow in the Orkneys, and in some maritime districts the shrub measures 9 feet tall and 15 feet across. The leaves, dark green above and white-felted beneath, are small, ovalish, the largest about 1 inch long. The flowers, small and Daisy-like, are white with yellow centres and come in flattish clusters; they bloom during July and August and have a delightful sweet Hawthorn scent. Like the rest of the family, the plant needs a lime-free, peaty soil, well drained, and a sunny situation.

*Pernettya* are closely akin to *Gaultheria* and like a cool, peaty soil as do the latter plants; but should be given a sunny spot. *Pernettya mucronata* and its varieties are the best known and the showiest of all the dwarf berrying evergreen shrubs we grow in this country. The leaves are very small, as are the white flowers. It is often impossible to see the foliage when the spreading branches are laden with berries – white, pink, crimson, red, purple or black – from autumn all through the winter months. There are many beautiful named varieties to choose from, and any nurseryman will supply a list. The plants are most effective when massed and give a magnificent show when associated with some of the autumn Crocuses and the taller, bigger Colchicums. (Male and female forms of the shrubs should be planted to ensure a good crop of berries.) The cost of a single plant is about half a guinea.

*Phlomis fruticosa* is the Jerusalem Sage which seems better known in some districts than in others. I've grown it in my garden for many years and lost it several times through frost. It is one of the grey-silver evergreens and needs a sheltered place in the London district. The plant makes a shrub about 3 feet tall here in South Bucks., with Sage-like, furry silvery leaves (the largest about 5 inches long and 2 inches wide), and clusters of bright yellow upright, hooded flowers. The plant is easily raised from cuttings; I always keep rooted cuttings in pots so that I can plant them out in spring. The plant is particularly charming when massed and also when grown with the purple-red flowered Rock-Rose, *Cistus X purpureus*.

*Pittosporum* are not seen in many inland gardens. When they are grown there, they are usually planted against a warm wall; but most people prefer to use what wall space they have for more valuable plants – those, say, that bear choice fruits, or beautiful flowers, The hardiest species is the New Zealand one called *P. tenuifolium*, yet it is nearly always grown near a wall in the London area. The plant has little floral beauty, and it is for its attractive evergreen foliage that it is grown. Indeed, sprays of it are much in demand by florists. In Cornwall and Southern Ireland it makes a tall bush or small tree 20 or 30 feet tall. The light green foliage makes the plant well worth growing. The flowers are small and of a purplish colour. Their chief attraction is their delightful honey-like fragrance. The shrub needs a good ordinary loamy soil.

*Skimmia* are low-growing shrubs which thrive in moist, loamy soils, where there is some shade. They are useful for a limited space, and *Skimmia japonica* is the one I have come across most frequently. It does well in town gardens – where there is but little shade, however; if the soil is moist, it will tolerate the sun on it apparently. The plant is grown solely for the bright red berries which follow the fragrant flowers. This shrub is not more than 3 or 4 feet tall and has yellowish-green leaves, usually 3 inches long and about 1 inch wide. The flowers, dull white and fragrant, come in terminal panicles in April. As male and female flowers are produced on different plants, it is necessary to grow both sexes together to ensure a good crop of berries.

*Vaccinium* are hardy shrubs but not commonly seen in gardens. They don't settle down well in ordinary soils and need moist leafmould or peat; they are useless in heavy soils containing lime.

The evergreen kinds are grown chiefly for their foliage or their fruits which come in autumn. Some have attractive flowers – *V. floribunda* (*mortinia*), for instance, with racemes of pink flowers in June (though these are partly hidden by the dark green foliage); moreover, this species is hardy only in the south and south-west of England.

The best of the genus for the average garden (in the Home Counties – not farther north, though) is *V. nummularia*, which makes a compact shrub, 9 inches high, with bright green leaves ½ inch to 1 inch long. The flowers in May are rose-red; the berries black and apparently edible.

*V. ovatum* is a tallish shrub, up to 10 feet high, with small, dark glossy green leaves, and white, bell-shaped flowers in May. The berries are black.

*V. vitis-idaea* (the native 'Cowberry' or 'Mountain Cranberry'), a low, creeping shrub, 6 to 10 inches high, with dark, lustrous green leaves like those of the Box, makes an excellent ground cover. The flowers, whitish-pink, come in early summer, and the bright red fruits in late autumn.

*V. myrtillus* is the Bilberry, which bears the small, bluish fruits used to make delicious tarts, especially in Yorkshire. It is common on the moors there, but doesn't settle down in gardens in the London district.

Another well-known species is the North-American *V. macrocarpum*, selected forms of which are grown for their fruits (the popular Cranberry we have at Christmas); vast acres in Canada and North America are specially cultivated for the production of the fruit. (The plant is often listed as *Oxycoccus macrocarpus*.) Both these fruiting species are extremely difficult, if not impossible, to establish in our gardens.

*Viburnum* on the whole are well known to gardeners; and the Laurustinus (*V. tinus*, described on page 44) is a favourite evergreen for screens and hedges. The deciduous species are the kinds mostly grown however; and these are the ones the majority of us have found easy to grow. The precocious *V. fragrans* which carries its richly scented flowers in winter is in my opinion the finest of all the species. The hybrid *V. X burkwoodii* (*V. carlesii* – deciduous, and *V. utile* – evergreen) has been neglected unfortunately, the reason being probably that it is considered to be rather tender. In the London district it does best against a wall; and in the south it seems to flower more freely in partial shade. A point in its favour is that it thrives well in town and city gardens, not minding at all a smoky, polluted atmosphere. The flowers, white, are deliciously fragrant and come in clusters about 4 inches across. They bloom early in the year, often opening in January. People who live in towns should certainly give this evergreen shrub a trial. Good specimens can be bought from any shrub nursery. The price is 17*s*. 6*d*. a plant.

There are many more evergreen shrubs as lovely as those I have described here, and many as rare. They are useless, however, grown outside in our inland gardens; and some even in the warm south need protection through severe weather. They might be termed connoisseur's plants; gardeners like to experiment with them, though they might regret the cost when the plants live only a year or two and regret more the loss of such lovely things.

3

Hardy evergreen climbing plants are extremely rare. The Common Ivy is probably the only truly reliable one. It grows practically anywhere – it would be difficult to find a plant that wasn't in a flourishing state. In places exposed to hot sun, it grows normally but usually becomes infested with pests such as the mealy-bug and caterpillars. Ivy climbs trees and buildings by means of aerial roots which form on the woody stems; and it also creeps over the ground and makes an excellent evergreen undergrowth. But it can be a nuisance when it is left uncontrolled. It should never be allowed to climb on a pergola (which it would soon cover and at the same time smother climbers more attractive), nor on valuable old buildings, the stone-work of which it would soon hide and eventually damage. Nothing could be more heinous than to plant it deliberately against the wall of some historic building famous for its beautifully-carved and intricate stone-work. Yet it can be used on some buildings with splendid effect. If it is kept carefully pruned back and not allowed to encroach on any fine architectural detail, it adds to the beauty of the stone-work and gives richness and colour to the structure. One never associates Ivy with any of our more rebarbative modern architecture. No one perhaps would think of planting it against a wall of cement, glass and steel.

The common species, *Hedera helix*, is a native of Europe and found in most parts of the British Isles. It grows to the top of trees 100 feet tall, and on mature specimens does no harm, though many gardeners believe it kills any tree once it reaches the top and the leafy growths and covers the bark completely; for it apparently stops the breathing functions of the tree. On the young trees it is nearly always a killer when it encircles the trunks and prevents normal growth.

When Ivy reaches the top of its support and ceases to climb, it changes its character and becomes productive, bearing flowers and berries, and larger, unlobed leaves. (See Fig. 11, showing the juvenile lobed leaves, and the adult unlobed leaves.)

The adult Ivy is known as the Bush or Tree Ivy, and is often cultivated as a shrub; it is quite an ornament in the garden with its clusters of greenish-yellow flowers during the autumn and later with its bunches of purple-black berries, which are the size of small peas.

*Fig.* 11. The Common Ivy

(*a*) Adult leaves with flowers

(*b*) Juvenile leaves and stem with aerial roots

The common plant has sported into an astonishing number of varieties, some with large leaves, some with smaller; others are beautifully variegated; yet others have differently and curiously shaped leaves.

The only one I grow in my garden is the common sort, which is planted as a ground cover in a shady place. It has the usual thick, leathery leaves, dark glossy green, with paler veins, and 3 or 5 deep lobes. When crushed the leaves give off an unpleasant smell.

I find that an occasional drastic clipping back of the leaves is beneficial (March is best), the new foliage that comes in May being naturally fresh-looking and clean. Ivies growing on buildings should always be clipped in this way: it keeps the plants free from pests and enables one to control the plant more easily.

The so-called Tree-Ivies are described under Var. ARBORESCENS. They are produced by cuttings of the flowering shoots of the common plant; and there are both silver and golden variegated kinds.

Var. AUREO-VARIEGATA is blotched with pale yellow, but is liable to revert. (AUREA-VARIÉGATA ARBORESCENS is the Bush form).

Var. DELTOIDEA has curiously-shaped leaves, the two basal lobes being rounded and overlapping.

Var. MARGINATA (a favourite variety, though I don't grow it) has its leaves broadly margined with creamy-white and tinged with pink during the winter. A lovely leaf. But like so many of the variegated kinds, it is liable to revert to the common green type after some years. It is wise therefore to renew them every so often, and it is easily done by cuttings or by layering.

Of the other species, *Helix hibernica*, is probably the best known; it is called the Irish Ivy and is said to be found wild in Ireland and the west of Scotland. The leaves are larger, and the plant makes a fine bush if it is kept well trimmed. It is not so hardy as the common sort but it grows and climbs more rapidly than that plant when given a wall as a support. (See also page 61.)

Although Ivy grows practically anywhere, in any ordinary soil, a new plant – especially one of the coloured varieties – should be started off in some good loam.

Honeysuckles (*Lonicera*) are favourite climbing or twining plants with most people. But probably only one evergreen species is hardy. This is *Lonicera japonica* which is grown in many gardens in the south and around London. I doubt, however, whether it would survive a very severe winter in this district if it were not planted against, and trained on, a wall. It is an excellent twiner for covering an old tree or some deciduous shrub which is not much valued – I've seen it twining round the rather brittle branches of the common *Buddleia davidii.* It would be better on an old apple tree, whose branches are stronger and better able to support the weight of the Honeysuckle after some years' growth, and it has made a dense tangle of stems. It has an extraordinarily long flowering season: it usually beings in early summer and during a mild spell will go on till late autumn. The flowers have a rich scent but they are not so striking as those of the leaf-shedding Honeysuckles we grow. They are creamy-white at first and change to yellow with age. The leaves are ovalish, the largest 3 inches long and a bright cheerful shade of green. Of the several forms of *Lonicera japonica* in cultivation, the best, certainly the most fragrant, is Var. HALLIANA.

The other evergreen climbers on the whole are more tender and something of a risk in many of our gardens. They require not only a warm wall but additional protection through the winter months.

Douglas Bartrum
Sunnyside
Bovingdon Green
MARLOW
BUCKS

# BIBLIOGRAPHY


Baker (H. C.) – ILLUSTRATIONS OF CONIFERS. (Hertford, 1909–13).

Bailey (L. H.) – THE CULTIVATION OF EVERGREENS. (London, 1923).

Bean (W. J.) – TREES AND SHRUBS HARDY IN THE BRITISH ISLES. (London, 1949).

Britton, Nathaniel Lord, and John A. Shafer – NORTH AMERICAN TREES. (New York, 1908).

Camellias and Magnolia: Conference Report. (R.H.S. London).

Carrière, Elie Abel – TRAITÉ GÉNÉRAL DES CONIFÉRES. (Paris).

Dallimore (W.) – HOLLY, YEW AND BOX. (London and New York, 1908).

Dallimore (W.) and Jackson (A. B.) HANDBOOK OF CONIFERAE. (London, 1923).

Dippel (L.) – HANDBUCH DER LAUBHOLZKUNDE. (Berlin).

Duhamel Du Monceau (Henri L.) – TRAITÉ DES ARBRES ET ARBUSTES. (Paris).

Eastwood, (A.) – A HANDBOOK OF THE TREES OF CALIFORNIA. (San Francisco, 1905).

Edlin, (H. L.) – BRITISH WOODLAND TREES. (London, 1944).

Elwes, (H. J.) and Augustine Henry – THE TREES OF GREAT BRITAIN AND IRELAND. (Edinburgh).

Forbes, (J.) – PINETUM WOBURNENSE; OR A CATALOGUE OF THE CONIFEROUS PLANTS IN THE COLLECTION OF THE DUKE OF BEDFORD AT WOBURN ABBEY. (London).

Hemsley (W. B.) – HANDBOOK OF HARDY TREES, SHRUBS, AND HERBACEOUS PLANTS. (Based on the French work of Messrs. Decaisne and Naudin). (London).

Hornibrook (M.) – DWARF AND SLOW-GROWING CONIFERS. (London, 1923).

Hume (H. H.) – CAMELLIAS IN AMERICA. (Pennsylvania).

Limpricht (W.) – BOTANISCHE REISEN IN DEN HOCHGEBIRGEN CHINAS UND OST-TIBETS. (Berlin, 1922).

Lowe (J.) – THE YEW TREES OF GREAT BRITAIN AND IRELAND. (London, 1897).

Millais (J. G.) – RHODODENRONS AND THEIR VARIOUS HYBRIDS. (London, 1917).

Millais (J. G.) – MAGNOLIAS. (London, 1927).

Mitford (A. B. F.) – (Lord Redesdale). – THE BAMBOO GARDEN. (London).

Murray (A.) – THE PINES AND FIRS OF JAPAN. (London, 1863).

Rehder (A.) – SYNOPSIS OF THE GENUS LONICERA. (St. Louis).

Rhododendron Society – THE SPECIES OF RHODODENDRON. (London).

R.H.S. Dictionary – (London).

Sargent (C. S.) – FOREST FLORA OF JAPAN. (Boston and New York).

Sealy (J. R.) – A REVISION OF THE GENUS CAMELLIA. (R.H.S. London).

Sweet (R.) – CISTINEAE. (London).

Thurston (E.) – TREES AND SHRUBS IN CORNWALL. (Cambridge).

Urquhart (B. L.) – THE CAMELLIA. (Urquhart Press).

Wertz (R.) – LES LYCIUM EUROPÉENS ET EXOTIQUES. (Paris).

Wilson (E. H.) and A. Rehder – A MONOGRAPH OF AZALEAS. (Cambridge, Mass.).

Yuccas – Mitteilungen an der deutschen dendrologischen Gesellschaft. (1920).

# Index